Pray for Justice

Thirty Days of Morning & Evening Prayer for Catholics and Other Peaceful People

Lou A. Bordisso, O.C.

"For everyone who asks receives; the one who seeks finds; and to the one who knocks, the door will be opened."
Matthew 7:8

APOCRYPHILE
PRESS

The Apocryphile Press
1700 Shattuck Ave. #81
Berkeley, CA 94709
www.apocryphile.org

Pray for Justice
Copyright © 2016 Lou A. Bordisso, O.C.
ISBN 978-1-944769-40-6

Printed in the United States of America

Dedication

This book is dedicated to guests of the Gubbio Project, homeless men and women who engage in sacred sleep in the pews and on the floor of St. Boniface Church in San Francisco, California. I am honored and privileged to serve among our homeless guests twice weekly as their chaplain. When I gaze into their eyes, I see the eyes of Jesus looking back at me.

Table of Contents

Introduction

You may already know the joy of peace and justice work and want to do more of it. But how can you find the time to do the work of God if you are among the many of us who are over-extended, over-worked and juggling competing values? How can you avoid burn-out and being unjust to yourself in the process of helping others?

You may already value contemplation, silence, and prayer as a way to nurture your own soul, connect with God, and help serve others. But sometimes, it seems impossible to get still enough, be un-busy and quiet enough for even a few moments of prayer. You may also be concerned about discerning the voice of God.

I share those concerns as a result of many years of peace and justice work in many venues. The best guidance I can give you is the suggestion to think about prayer, peace and justice work not just as more things to fit into your daily routine. Rather, view prayer as your sustaining source, your interior foundation and preparation for external works of mercy and charity you do as you go about your day.

Whether you are Catholic, a former Catholic, a member of another faith or "spiritual but not religious,' you can learn and be inspired by the long history of Catholic peace and justice teachings and practices. Many of these practices and teachings come from monastic orders, all of which ordered their work and life around prayer throughout the day.

Here is an example from my own life:

"Preach by deeds, and if necessary, use words," is one of my favorite instructions from St. Francis of Assisi. Whenever I followed this dictum, I was amazed at how important our presence, not just our presents, were to the people we served.

One year, a project I was involved in gave out hand-knitted scarves, each boxed and wrapped by volunteers. One teenager walked about a half block away before opening his gift. Ecstatic, he ran back to me and said it was the first Christmas gift he was ever given in his life. He then kissed me on the cheek before running down the street into the darkness of a foggy and cold night.

Another time, I was impressed by a man who would not take whatever services I was offering until he told me his name and saw that I honored him as a person.[1]

Over the years and in the course of ministry, I learned that peace and justice work is about mirroring God's love in the present, everyday, ordinary moment. Often these moments lead to extraordinary expressions of charity and mercy.

Many of us believe that for peace and justice work to be successful, it must always be done in a way that is extraordinary or excessive. In that sense, "labor of love" can easily turn into an obsession or martyrdom, neither of which serves us or those who need our services.

One of my favorite guidelines is, "Strive for simplicity in your peace and justice work." As St. Francis once said, "While you are proclaiming peace with your lips, be careful to have it even more fully in your heart." If you're not sure whether your words or actions are good or bad, right or wrong, simply ask yourself if your heart is at peace. A peaceful heart can be a helpful measuring stick.

Another favorite guideline comes from St. Teresa: "When you are too busy to pray...you are too busy." There are so many opportunities to do peace and justice work, once we recognize the needs of those in our immediate midst who are hurting. We can make a huge difference when we simply speak out for those who have no voice at a parish council meeting, reach out to a marginalized colleague at the office, or visit a sick friend. We can always reach out to a "black sheep" family member who is being ignored and living in exile.

---

1   A more complete telling of the scarf story and other experiences are told later in this section.

These are just a few of the everyday opportunities to reflect God's goodness and kindness in the world. Each opportunity fulfilled can lead to big changes. Consider the child who struggles with homework. Choose to ignore that child, and you may add to his or her discouragement and frustration. Scream out how s/he a worthless loser, and you help cripple his or her ability to know and do the best. Listen to children's challenges, celebrate their successes and simply bless them with your presence, and you help those children thrive. With your caring goes a bit more confidence and courage to help them find their own ways to love themselves and others, hence, a concrete exercise of peace and justice.

St. Benedict instructed his monks to "work and pray." People of all faiths have increasingly found that any work can be done so that work and prayer are not mutually exclusive, but complementary. Thus, work-life balance for peace and justice work, nourished by prayer, can be a reality in this hectic world. A big part of the stress-free equation is to embody and value your kindness, then take time to treasure the gifts you receive as you give.

Pray for Justice: 30 Days of Morning and Evening Prayer for Catholics and Other Peaceful People is intended and designed as a practical prayer book for busy people who are seeking to maintain equilibrium between work and prayer. This book recognizes that – in addition to the "normal" stresses of life and work – peace and justice work may invite you to consider doing tasks in a dangerous or unharmonious condition. It recognizes that, desperate as they are for practical help, those we serve are just as in need of attentive caring, even when we are exhausted by all the undertakings that are essential when serving and mirroring Christ in ordinary life.

God's concern for the poor and marginalized is revealed through transformation of our human hearts. This requires an intimate and loving relationship with God, which requires prayer time. Taking time for prayer can awaken a sense of relatedness, mutuality, inter-dependence, and collaboration with God.

Religious training and experience teach me that when we are in love with God, love from God manifests in our hearts, then it is expressed through our lives. Our relationship with God mirrors our relationships with other humans just as our relationship with other people mirrors our relationship with God. Ultimately, the goodness and kindness of God is revealed through roles of service while we are in solidarity with the least among us.

We simply cannot love that which we do not know and does not know us in return. God's love for humankind and the ministry of peace and justice with the least among us is a mutual effort of redemption. This is how participating in peace and justice work helps build the Reign of God. Ideally, peace and social justice are stimulated as human freedom grows and matures with a fundamental option for God. According to Father Richard McBrien, this means, "The radical orientation of one's whole life toward or away from God. [It is] akin to conversion. The moral concept is directly opposed to legalism... which focuses on the morality of individual acts."[2]

My hope is that *Pray for Justice* helps to plant a seed for daily prayer that will sprout and flourish so that we may encounter and serve the face of Jesus in all our work.

Prayerful Lessons from a Lifetime of Peace and Justice Work. Because many of us learn best from experience and stories, I offer a few examples of how this has worked out for me, often when it was least expected. Hopefully these stories will help stir your own ideas and memories of how precious caring and prayer are to you.

My peace and justice work began many moons ago as a civilian employee with the Department of the Navy, followed by four years of studying at the Franciscan School of Theology at the Graduate Theological Union in Berkeley, California. During that time, while I still in formation with my Roman Catholic religious order, I was immersed in the challenges of living in a third-world country, followed by participation in two San Francisco Peace and Social Justice groups: Religious Witness with Homeless People and Father Francis Homeless Program. After retirement, I have worked with St. Anthony's Dining Room, the Gubbio Project, Alzheimer's advocacy services and for LGBT equality and justice.

---

2   McBrien, Richard P. *Catholicism* (NY: HarperSanFrancisco, 1966) p. 1240

Encountering the Face of Jesus while Employed by the Department of Defense. Roughly four times a year I traveled abroad as an Employee Assistance Program Administrator and Counseling Psychologist to provide shore side counseling and educational services to civilian employees in various Asian and Southeast Asian ports of call.

My most frequent destination was Subic Bay Navy Base in the Philippines. Often, after work, I walked across a bridge to Olongapo City for an evening meal. One night I was returning to the base when I noticed a beggar sitting on the bridge's pedestrian walkway holding a small wicker basket. His or her arms were stretched out, hoping someone would toss a coin in the basket.

I say him or her because the person's whole body was covered with some sort of fabric; only the whites of the eyes were visible. As I tossed my coin into the basket, the head of the beggar nodded up and down as if communicating "yes" while looking at me with piercing eyes. My heart was overwhelmed with joy, and my eyes filled with tears. I have absolutely no doubt that the eyes of Jesus were gazing back at me.

This brief and overwhelming exchange unexpectedly and abruptly inspired me to journey among and serve those who are in need, outcast, or marginalized in any way. Since then, I have found many ways to simply and joyously serve others.

Immersed in the Hungry Face of Jesus in a Third-world Country. During the third year of my M.Div. study at the Franciscan School of Theology, I was elated to return to the Philippines for my immersion practicum.

One night the parish at New Manila, where I lived, had a festival in their social hall. As I ate, I noticed that many malnourished children were observing us from the outside but were not invited to join us. When the feast ended and the last person left the social hall, I invited the children in and had them sit at the tables. I did not ask anyone for permission to give the children the food that remained on the buffet table.

Word must have spread quickly among the children because before I knew it, every seat at every table was filled! I happily served each of them. Though plate portions had to be small enough to provide enough food to many hungry mouths, everybody got enough. Multiplication of the loaves, anyone?

As far as I know, the parish pastoral staff either chose to remain silent and not reprimand me or I was not on their radar screen. Had there been a reprimand, I was prepared to follow the old maxim: sometimes it is better to ask for forgiveness than permission!

Encountering the Face of Jesus Among Homeless People. Religious Witness with Homeless People was founded by a nun to advocate for and support shelterless people who slept on the streets of San Francisco. During my involvement, local government officials were cracking down on those sleeping in doorways, in parks, or on public or private property. The police were known to badger homeless men and women in the middle of the night, wake them up, and make them move. Police sometimes confiscated sleeping bags or blankets.

To counter this appalling police conduct, religious and lay folks slept among the homeless in large groups, resolving to keep the police from disturbing the homeless as they quietly slept. On at least two occasions, we invited those without shelter to sleep with us on the steps of City Hall and in Golden Gate Park as an expression of protest. We provided sleeping bags as needed.

The police were notified of our non-violent protest beforehand. The two nights we slept among the homeless, the police came but did not approach our camp. They allowed all gathered to rest without maltreatment.

A favorite prayer says, *"May God guide us while we are awake and guard us while we sleep, that sleeping or waking we may be faithful to Christ."* That night, God granted all gathered a "peaceful night and a perfect end."

Encountering the Face of Jesus During Civil Disobedience. Sometimes as we planned non-violent civil disobedience protests, we expected to be arrested so we could challenge oppressive homeless laws through the judicial system. Sometimes we made a legal dent; other times, not so much. Twice I was arrested with several religious nuns, brothers, and priests.

One arrest happened in San Francisco's Union Square, which did not allow sitting or sleeping from dusk to morning, so we simply sat on the ground. One by one the police hauled us off in handcuffs and issued citations. It was amazing how the officers treated women religious in habits with respect and gentleness as they were being handcuffed and cited. I assume those officers were Catholic. Maybe sometimes "Catholic guilt" plays a constructive role!

At another protest, we wanted vacant housing at a closed military base to be opened to those without shelter. After many rejections from public officials on this matter, both Religious Witness with Homeless People and those living on the streets occupied one building on federal land with the intention of bringing the housing question to federal court.

As we were hauled away in handcuffs in the paddy wagon singing, *"We Shall Overcome,"* I was overwhelmed as I recalled the words in the Magnificat, "God has cast down the mighty from their thrones and has lifted up the lowly…God has filled the hungry with good things, and the rich he sent away empty."

Later, my spiritual director asked me, "Where is God in all this?" I responded, "God was in solidarity with the lowly and was made visible through our minds, bodies, and souls."

A Casual Walk Leads to the Father Francis Homeless Project. The Tenderloin section of San Francisco is known for being a dangerous place where drug dealers, drug buyers and the needy walk the streets day and night. As a lay member of my former religious order and I walked those streets one night, we wondered: How could we best serve the many faces of Jesus there?

A few days later we returned with a grocery cart full of potato chips and personal care items. We were amazed by the conversations we had and how receptive people were to our presence.

On return visits, we were astonished at the number of children and teens on the streets of San Francisco. Most had come to the City for refuge from an abusive home or having been kicked out of home with no place to go. The rest were runaways. The closer we got to the Polk-Gulch district of San Francisco (adjacent to the Tenderloin), the more homeless youth we discovered. After many touching but brief encounters with street children followed by prayer and prudent discernment, we realized God was beckoning us to concentrate our ministry in this district.

The homeless youth were requesting socks for their feet and blankets to help them stay warm as they slept in alleyways and doorways on cold and chilly nights.

As word got around, enough donations came to our new Father Francis Homeless Project to form a nonprofit organization and buy a second-hand van. That helped us distribute more blankets, socks, and donated jackets. Eventually, I cooked a few large pots of spaghetti in the kitchen of the convent where I lived to serve our youthful friends.

Providing food, blankets, socks, and jackets became one of the most heartwarming points in my life. It became a connecting point for us to provide a listening ear and warm heart. Always, we provided a ministry of presence. Simply because we were there, the kids knew someone cared about them just as they are and with no hidden agendas.

It was at the Father Francis Homeless Project that the young teenager was so ecstatic to receive his first ever Christmas gift. That night, I saw Jesus masquerading as a hurting street kid. I marveled at how joyfully gold, frankincense, and myrrh masqueraded as a simple scarf.

Encountering the Face of Jesus After Retirement. A few years ago, I was diagnosed with Younger Onset and Early Stage Alzheimer's and Lewy Body Disease with Parkinson's symptoms. Due to my diagnosis, I took an early retirement. These days much of my time is spent volunteering as an advocate for Alzheimer's. While the advocacy work has been rewarding, something was missing.

Then I saw a news report on a local television station about St. Anthony's Dining Room in San Francisco. The spokesperson said they get plenty of volunteers during the holiday season, but volunteers were needed year-round. Immediately, I applied. Given my pastoral care background and mental health provider experience, I was assigned to the social service Information and Referral table in the dining room, where once again I could engage directly with those in need.

Although I only volunteered a few hours a week, I was at the right place at the right time in my life. Each week, after my volunteer service at St. Anthony's Dining Room, I walked next door to St. Boniface Church to meditate, reflect, and pray. Posted there is a quote from Pope Francis in large letters,

> *"I prefer a church which is bruised, hurting, and dirty because it has been out on the streets, rather than a church which is unhealthy from being confined and from clinging to its own security. I do not want a church concerned with being at the center and then ends up by being caught up in a web of obsessions and procedures."*

St. Boniface Church, in the middle of a very poor area of San Francisco, can easily be described as bruised, hurting, and dirty. In many ways it is a reflection of the homeless men and women who find in its Gubbio Project a peaceful sanctuary for rest during the day.

The Project offers "sacred sleep," filling the pews and floor space throughout the church. When I pray among those who are engaged in sacred sleep, I am blessed to be in such a holy dwelling place. The sounds of snoring and the stench of body odors may fill the air, but the heavenly scent of incense refreshes the church. In this sanctified space I am reminded that I am blessed to be among the Body of Christ. My heart is often stirred to the point of tears.

When I was being interviewed for the Gubbio chaplaincy, I was asked why I wanted to volunteer. Without hesitation, I responded by saying, *"It is where my heard is, I encounter God."* Today, my volunteer Gubbio chaplain homeless ministry provides me a chance to bring to the table a warm heart, smile, and a listening ear.

Insights from Catholic Peace and Justice. The Roman Catholic Church has gradually evolved and articulated her social doctrine teachings dating back to the papacy of Pope Leo XIII (1881).[3] Generally, Catholic social doctrine invites us to consider the proposition of the Gospel in matters concerning social justice, peace, and human rights. Ultimately, Catholic social teachings may help us dis-

---

3   Pope Leo XIII *Rerum Novarum (encyclical)* (1891) p. 672

cern how justice is practiced and applied to our culture, politics, and modern economics.

Catholic social justice teachings proclaim that a rudimentary measuring stick for morals and virtues is to ask ourselves how our most vulnerable members are faring. Today, the gap grows between rich and poor. However, the social doctrine teaching of our church challenges us to recall the biblical instructions of *Matthew 25* by inviting us to consider and advocate first for the needs of the poor, helpless, frail, and impoverished.

One way our loving and compassionate God communicates is through human efforts and works of mercy directed toward building the Reign of God. It should come as no surprise that the apostle James insists that we Christians ought to be *"doers and not simply hearers of the word"* in our works of mercy among the poor, the oppressed and outcast. Through the transformation of our hearts as gradually revealed in our works of mercy, God's concern for the poor and marginalized shines forth!

Ultimately, our quest for peace and justice and building the Reign of God flows from our deep and loving relationship with our God. God's invitation, therefore, often requires us to challenge unjust and oppressive social systems through our endeavor to reveal the goodness and kindness of God. By our roles of service and solidarity among the People of God, peace and justice are more fully realized and we are more committed to a fundamental option for the poor and for God. When we embrace a fundamental option for God and the impoverished, poverty-stricken, and destitute, God's justice and peace cannot help but be reflected and mirrored in our daily life.

My sincere hope is that *Pray for Justice* will serve as a source of affirmation and challenge for those involved with peace and justice already and as an inspiring guide for those seeking the path God is inviting them to here and now. I invite you to see this book as an invitation to walk through a doorway to your path with the resolve to mirror the goodness and kindness of God our Savior by all ways and means.

Finally, while on your journey, remember the words of St. Augustine, "*If you are seeking, you have already been found.*" Then enjoy the fellowship of many companions you will get to know on your faith journey, as we all continue to seek and discover God's will for us.

A Helpful Guide for 30 Days
of Morning and Evening Prayer

❖

Foundation for this Guide. This book is built on the foundation of the Evangelical Counsels, which you may know as the vows of Poverty, Chastity, and Obedience. These Counsels have been newly interpreted, reframed, and reiterated for ordinary everyday life. The Evangelical Counsels can serve as an underlying principle not only for praying this book but also as a practical way of imitating Christ within the context of Peace and Social Justice:

Poverty is not so much about living in destitution, but an intention to live simply so others can simply live. Intended Simplicity of Life invites sharing what we have; being good stewards of our time, talent, and treasure; and striving to liberate ourselves by living with what we need and not what we want.

Chastity is not so much about sex and sexuality as it is having Purity of Heart. This means having the disposition and attitude of respect for ourselves and others. Purity of Heart strives to live a life of virtue by finding a "middle-way" between excesses. It means joyfully making personal sacrifices in order to accomplish a moral good and to practice life-giving and affirming relationships.

Obedience is not so much about obeying an authority as it is active listening and being informed by – not dictated to – external authorities, whether they be political, religious, family, national, or any institutional external voices. Active Listening means exercising Primacy of Conscience, with intention for the common good, even if our conscience might be in error. Ultimately, obedience means listening to the gentle voice of God while being prudent, prayerful, and discerning.

Simplicity of Life, Purity of Heart, and Active Listening are core principles underlying the tradition and spirituality of Catholic Peace and Justice. These principles are less concerned with rules and laws and more about living a moral life of virtue and character grounded in the intent to love God, neighbor, world, and self.

Guidelines for Working with this Book. The intent of this helpful guide is to propose and not impose ways to pray.

Time and location. Before you begin your daily prayers, pray for clarity to create your best rhythm of prayer. To the best possible extent, pray at the same time daily, selecting times that best foster your sense of serenity and when you are most attentive. Designate a sacred location that will minimize disturbances and distractions. Some people like to pray in a secluded place in their garden or a quiet room in the house such as bedroom, living room – even the bathroom, if there are no other options for solitude.

A Moment of Silence. In the beginning of each prayer time, be silent to center yourself, focus, and settle in to prayer. Some people prefer only a moment of silence; others take ten to twenty minutes. Depending on your level of comfort, you might begin with a short period of silence and over the course of 30 days, extend the amount of time in silence.

Peace and Justice Quote. Read and pray the quote of the day slowly and deliberately. Read, pray, and ponder the words a second or third time, if need be. Read more with your heart than with your mind. Note without judgment if you are resistant and defensive or accepting and receptive to the quote. Then let go and surrender to the illumination of God in your midst.

Morning and Evening Prayers. The morning and evening prayer configuration is in the spirit of the ancient tradition of the Church blended in a post-modern style with the explicit intention to keep the format simple.

Prayer in the morning. Morning Prayer incorporates a moment of silence, an opening prayer, a peace and justice quote, Canticle of Zechariah, a prayerful intention for the day, the Lord's Prayer, and a closing prayer. It invites you to consider what our God of peace and justice might be inviting you to explore or act on today and resolve to respond in the spirit of collaboration, mutuality, and inter-dependence.

Prayer in the evening. As the day comes to a close, re-read the prayer in light of how your day unfolded. Evening Prayer incorporates a moment of silence, an opening prayer, a peace and justice quote, a repeat of the morning prayerful intention, Canticle of Mary, Examination of Conscience, Act of Contrition, Hail Mary, and closing prayer.

Examination of Conscience. Review the course of your day. Ask yourself if you trusted in God and did your part. Consider your sins of omission and commission. In light of your intention and resolve, honestly acknowledge what you have done and what you failed to do and what you said or failed to say. Sincerely ask yourself what you could improve in light of the theme of the peace and justice quote and your intentions.

Act of Contrition. With a contrite heart, share with God your regrets and sorrow. Affirm that you will strive, with the help of God's grace, to avoid missing the mark and avoid further digressions and distractions from God's mercy and compassion.

Canticle of Zechariah (morning) and **Canticle of Mary** (evening): Pray the opening and closing prayers and **Canticles** with authenticity, faithfulness, and sincerity. Avoid rushing through the prayers and **Canticles**. Contemplate the words and phrases and their meaning for you here and now. Allow enough time for soul-searching and reflection.

Peace and Justice Journal. A brief spiritual journal follows both morning and evening prayer where you can record your thoughts and insights and return to them later, time and time again, if desired. As with all of the above suggestions, the journal writing is optional. The hope for the morning journal is to focus on what you believe God is asking you to initiate in thought, word, and/or deed for that day. It stresses personal introspection and musing, as well as consideration for peace and justice intentions for the day. The spiritual journal following evening prayer stresses a scrutiny of the day. It invites you to reflect on how you responded to God's invitation as the day unfolded, what you might consider doing differently, and what you could do better, if needed.

Prayer Practice Habits for Consideration. Avoid scrupulosity. Make every effort not to judge yourself. Shy away from lofty expectations for yourself.

Finally, strive not to be excessively dependent on God or excessively independent from God in the ordinary practice of peace and justice. Cultivate an attitude and disposition of collaboration, mutuality, and inter-dependence *with* God.

30 Days of Prayer

Day One: Morning Prayer

Please take a moment of silence and quiet time.

Opening Prayer

O God, open my lips, and my mouth will proclaim your praise.

Peace and Social Justice Quote

In the twilight of life, God will not judge us on our earthly possessions and human success, but rather on how much we have loved.

— St. John of the Cross

Prayer

Loving God, help me to increase my love for others today – especially the vulnerable and marginalized – rather than love for my
possessions and material goods.

Please take a short period of time to contemplate the quote.

Canticle of Zechariah

Blessed are you, O God, for you have turned to your people and
saved us and set us free. You have raised up for us a strong deliverer, and so you promised: age after age you proclaimed by the lips
of your holy prophets that you would deliver us, calling to mind
your solemn covenant. This was the promise that you made: to
rescue us and free us from fear, so that we might worship you with
a holy worship, in your holy presence our whole life long. In your

tender compassion, the morning sun has risen upon us – to shine on us in our darkness, to guide our feet into the paths of peace.

Our Father

Our Father, who art in heaven, hallowed be your name; your kingdom come; your will be done on earth as it is in heaven. Give us this day our daily bread; and forgive us our trespasses as we forgive those who trespass against us; and lead us not into temptation, but deliver us from evil. Amen.

Closing Prayer

May God be gracious to me, show me kindness, and fill my heart with peace.

Spiritual Journal

My peace and social justice intent for today:

Day One: Evening Prayer

Please take a moment of silence and quiet time.

Opening Prayer

God, come to my assistance. Holy One, make haste to help me.

Peace and Social Justice Quote

In the twilight of life, God will not judge us on our earthly possessions and human success, but rather on how much we have loved.

—St. John of the Cross

Prayer

Loving God, help me to increase my love for others today – especially the vulnerable and marginalized – rather than love for my possessions and material goods.

Please take a short period of time to contemplate the quote.

Canticle of Mary

Our souls proclaim the glory of the Holy One; our spirits rejoice in God, our Savior, for you have looked with favor upon your lowly servant. You have done great things and holy is your name. You have cast down the mighty, and lifted up the lowly; you have filled the hungry with good things, and have sent the rich away empty. You have come to your children and set them free, for you have remembered your promise of mercy to our mothers and fathers, and to all your children forever.

Examination of Conscience

How have I loved the vulnerable and marginalized today? What could I do better?

Act of Contrition

Most merciful God, we confess that we have sinned against you in thought, word, and deed, by what we have done, and by what we have left undone. We have not loved you with our whole heart; we have not loved our neighbors as ourselves. We are truly sorry and we humbly repent. For the sake of your Son Jesus Christ, have mercy on us and forgive us; that we may delight in your will, and walk in your ways, to the glory of your Name. Amen.

Hail Mary

Hail Mary, full of grace. The Lord is with you. Blessed art you amongst women, and blessed is the fruit of your womb, Jesus. Holy Mary, Mother of God, pray for us sinners, now and at the hour of our death. Amen.

Closing Prayer

May God grant me a peaceful night and a perfect end. May the divine assistance be always with me and with all my loved ones.

Spiritual Journal

What have I done, what have I failed to do today? What have I said, what have I failed to say today? What could I do better?

Day Two: Morning Prayer

Please take a moment of silence and quiet time.

Opening Morning Prayer

O God, open my lips, and my mouth will proclaim your praise.

Peace and Social Justice Quote

When someone steals another's clothes, we call them a thief. Should we not give the same name to one who could clothe the naked and does not? The bread in your cupboard belongs to the hungry; the coat hanging unused in your closet belongs to the one who needs it; the shoes rotting in your closet belong to the one who has no shoes; the money which you hoard up belongs to the poor.

—Basil the Great

Prayer

Merciful God, teach me to take seriously my responsibility to ensure that persons in need are realized.

Please take a short period of time to contemplate the quote.

Canticle of Zechariah

Blessed be God who has turned to his people and saved us and set us free. You have raised up for us a strong deliverer, and so you promised: age after age you proclaimed by the lips of your holy prophets that you would deliver us, calling to mind your solemn covenant. This was the promise that you made: to rescue us and free us from fear, so that we might worship you with a holy worship, in your holy presence our whole life long. In your tender compassion, the morning sun has risen upon us – to shine on us in our darkness, to guide our feet into the paths of peace.

Our Father

Our Father, who art in heaven, hallowed be your name; your kingdom come; your will be done on earth as it is in heaven. Give us this day our daily bread; and forgive us our trespasses as we forgive those who trespass against us; and lead us not into temptation, but deliver us from evil. Amen.

Closing Prayer

May God be gracious to me, show me kindness, and fill my heart with peace.

Spiritual Journal

My peace and social justice intent for today:

Day Two: Evening Prayer

Please take a moment of silence and quiet time.

Opening Prayer

God, come to my assistance. Holy One, make haste to help me.

Peace and Social Justice Quote

When someone steals another's clothes, we call them a thief. Should we not give the same name to one who could clothe the naked and does not? The bread in your cupboard belongs to the hungry; the coat hanging unused in your closet belongs to the one who needs it; the shoes rotting in your closet belong to the one who has no shoes; the money which you hoard up belongs to the poor.

—Basil the Great

Please take a short period of time to contemplate the quote.

Canticle of Mary

Our souls proclaim the glory of the Holy One; our spirits rejoice in God, our Savior, for you have looked with favor upon your lowly servant. You have done great things and holy is your name. You have cast down the mighty, and lifted up the lowly; you have filled the hungry with good things, and have sent the rich away empty. You have come to your children and set them free, for you have remembered your promise of mercy to our mothers and fathers, and to all your children forever.

Prayer

Merciful God, teach me to take seriously my responsibility to ensure that persons in need are realized.

Examination of Conscience

How have I helped someone in need today? What could I do better?

Act of Contrition

Most merciful God, we confess that we have sinned against you in thought, word, and deed, by what we have done, and by what we have left undone. We have not loved you with our whole heart; we have not loved our neighbors as ourselves. We are truly sorry and we humbly repent. For the sake of your Son Jesus Christ, have mercy on us and forgive us; that we may delight in your will, and walk in your ways, to the glory of your Name. Amen.

Hail Mary

Hail Mary, full of grace. The Lord is with you. Blessed are you amongst women, and blessed is the fruit of your womb, Jesus. Holy Mary, Mother of God, pray for us sinners, now and at the hour of our death. Amen.

Closing Prayer

May God grant me a peaceful night and a perfect end. May the divine assistance be always with me and with all my loved ones.

Spiritual Journal

What have I done, what have I failed to do today? What have I said, what have I failed to say today? What could I do better?

Day Three: Morning Prayer

Please take a moment of silence and quiet time.

Opening Prayer

O God, open my lips, and my mouth will proclaim your praise.

Peace and Social Justice Quote

Violence is a lie, for it goes against the truth of our faith, the truth of our humanity.

—Saint John Paul II

Prayer

Peaceful God, grace me with the resolve to love and serve humankind with increasing peace in my heart, on my lips, and on my mind.

Please take a short period of time to contemplate the quote.

Canticle of Zechariah

Blessed are you, O God, for you have turned to your people and saved us and set us free. You have raised up for us a strong deliverer, and so you promised: age after age you proclaimed by the lips of your holy prophets that you would deliver us, calling to mind your solemn covenant. This was the promise that you made: to rescue us and free us from fear, so that we might worship you with a holy worship, in your holy presence our whole life long. In your

tender compassion, the morning sun has risen upon us – to shine on us in our darkness, to guide our feet into the paths of peace.

Our Father

Our Father, who art in heaven, hallowed be your name; your kingdom come; your will be done on earth as it is in heaven. Give us this day our daily bread; and forgive us our trespasses as we forgive those who trespass against us; and lead us not into temptation, but deliver us from evil. Amen.

Closing Prayer

May God be gracious to me, show me kindness, and fill my heart with peace.

Spiritual Journal

My peace and social justice intent for today:

Day Three: Evening Prayer

Please take a moment of silence and quiet time.

Opening Prayer

God, come to my assistance. Holy One, make haste to help me.

Peace and Social Justice Quote

Violence is a lie, for it goes against the truth of our faith, the truth of our humanity.

—Saint John Paul II

Please take a short period of time to contemplate the quote.

Canticle of Mary

Our souls proclaim the glory of the Holy One; our spirits rejoice in God, our savior, for you have looked with favor upon your lowly servant. You have done great things and holy is your name. You have cast down the mighty, and lifted up the lowly; you have filled the hungry with good things, and have sent the rich away empty. You have come to your children and set them free, for you have remembered your promise of mercy to our mothers and fathers, and to all your children forever.

Prayer

Peaceful God, grace me with the resolve to love and serve humankind with increasing peace in my heart, on my lips, and on my mind.

Examination of Conscience

Did I have peace in my heart, on my lips, and on my mind today? What could I do better?

Act of Contrition

Most merciful God, we confess that we have sinned against you in thought, word, and deed, by what we have done, and by what we have left undone. We have not loved you with our whole heart; we have not loved our neighbors as ourselves. We are truly sorry and we humbly repent. For the sake of your Son Jesus Christ, have mercy on us and forgive us; that we may delight in your will, and walk in your ways, to the glory of your Name. Amen.

Hail Mary

Hail Mary, full of grace. The Lord is with you. Blessed are you amongst women, and blessed is the fruit of your womb, Jesus. Holy Mary, Mother of God, pray for us sinners, now and at the hour of our death. Amen.

Closing Prayer

May God grant me a peaceful night and a perfect end. May the divine assistance be always with me and with all my loved ones.

Spiritual Journal

What have I done, what have I failed to do today? What have I said, what have I failed to say today? What could I do better?

Day Four: Morning Prayer

Please take a moment of silence and quiet time.

Opening Prayer

O God, open my lips, and my mouth will proclaim your praise.

Peace and Social Justice Quote

The only thing we can offer to God of value is to give our love to people as unworthy of it as we are to God's love.

—St. Catherine of Siena

Prayer

Caring God, assist me in my awareness of global inequality and my efforts to cultivate my duty to give my love to people I consider unworthy.

Please take a short period of time to contemplate the quote.

Canticle of Zechariah

Blessed are you, O God, for you have turned to your people and saved us and set us free. You have raised up for us a strong deliverer, and so you promised: age after age you proclaimed by the lips of your holy prophets that you would deliver us, calling to mind your solemn covenant. This was the promise that you made: to rescue us and free us from fear, so that we might worship you with a holy worship, in your holy presence our whole life long. In your

tender compassion, the morning sun has risen upon us – to shine on us in our darkness, to guide our feet into the paths of peace.

Our Father

Our Father, who art in heaven, hallowed be your name; your kingdom come; your will be done on earth as it is in heaven. Give us this day our daily bread; and forgive us our trespasses as we forgive those who trespass against us; and lead us not into temptation, but deliver us from evil. Amen.

Closing Prayer

May God be gracious to me, show me kindness, and fill my heart with peace.

Spiritual Journal

My peace and social justice intent for today:

Day Four: Evening Prayer

Please take a moment of silence and quiet time.

Opening Prayer

God, come to my assistance. Holy One, make haste to help me.

Peace and Social Justice Quote

The only thing we can offer to God of value is to give our love to people as unworthy of it as we are to God's love.

—St. Catherine of Siena

Prayer

Caring God, assist me in my awareness of global inequality and my efforts to cultivate my duty to give my love to people I consider unworthy.

Please take a short period of time to contemplate the quote.

Canticle of Mary

Our souls proclaim the glory of the Holy One; our spirits rejoice in God, our Savior, for you have looked with favor upon your lowly servant. You have done great things and holy is your name. You have cast down the mighty, and lifted up the lowly; you have filled the hungry with good things, and have sent the rich away empty. You have come to your children and set them free, for you have

remembered your promise of mercy to our mothers and fathers, and to all your children forever.

Examination of Conscience

In what ways did I love someone that I considered unworthy of my love today? What could I do better?

Act of Contrition

Most merciful God, we confess that we have sinned against you in thought, word, and deed, by what we have done, and by what we have left undone. We have not loved you with our whole heart; we have not loved our neighbors as ourselves. We are truly sorry and we humbly repent. For the sake of your Son Jesus Christ, have mercy on us and forgive us; that we may delight in your will, and walk in your ways, to the glory of your Name. Amen.

Hail Mary

Hail Mary, full of grace. The Lord is with you. Blessed are you amongst women, and blessed is the fruit of your womb, Jesus. Holy Mary, Mother of God, pray for us sinners, now and at the hour of our death. Amen.

Closing Prayer

May God grant me a peaceful night and a perfect end. May the divine assistance be always with me and with all my loved ones.

Spiritual Journal

What have I done, what have I failed to do today? What have I said, what have I failed to say today? What could I do better?

Day Five: Morning Prayer

Please take a moment of silence and quiet time.

Opening Prayer

O God, open my lips, and my mouth will proclaim your praise.

Peace and Social Justice Quote

Acquire inward peace, and a multitude around you will find salvation.

—St. Seraphim

Prayer

Gentle God, lead me to inner peace, calm, and serenity.

Please take a short period of time to contemplate the quote.

Canticle of Zechariah

Blessed are you, O God, for you have turned to your people and saved us and set us free. You have raised up for us a strong deliverer, and so you promised: age after age you proclaimed by the lips of your holy prophets that you would deliver us, calling to mind your solemn covenant. This was the promise that you made: to rescue us and free us from fear, so that we might worship you with a holy worship, in your holy presence our whole life long. In your tender compassion, the morning sun has risen upon us – to shine on us in our darkness, to guide our feet into the paths of peace.

Our Father

Our Father, who art in heaven, hallowed be your name; your kingdom come; your will be done on earth as it is in heaven. Give us this day our daily bread; and forgive us our trespasses as we forgive those who trespass against us; and lead us not into temptation, but deliver us from evil. Amen.

Closing Prayer

May God be gracious to me, show me kindness, and fill my heart with peace.

Spiritual Journal

My peace and social justice intent for today:

Day Five: Evening Prayer

Please take a moment of silence and quiet time.

Opening Prayer

God, come to my assistance. Holy One, make haste to help me.
Peace and Social Justice Quote Acquire inward peace, and a multitude around you will find salvation.

—St. Seraphim

Prayer

Gentle God, lead me to inner peace, calm, and serenity.

Please take a short period of time to contemplate the quote.

Canticle of Mary

Our souls proclaim the glory of the Holy One; our spirits rejoice in God, our Savior, for you have looked with favor upon your lowly servant. You have done great things and holy is your name. You have cast down the mighty, and lifted up the lowly; you have filled the hungry with good things, and have sent the rich away empty. You have come to your children and set them free, for you have remembered your promise of mercy to our mothers and fathers, and to all your children forever.

Examination of Conscience

What steps have I taken that would lead me to inner peace, calm, and serenity today? What could I do better?

Act of Contrition

Most merciful God, we confess that we have sinned against you in thought, word, and deed, by what we have done, and by what we have left undone. We have not loved you with our whole heart; we have not loved our neighbors as ourselves. We are truly sorry and we humbly repent. For the sake of your Son Jesus Christ, have mercy on us and forgive us; that we may delight in your will, and walk in your ways, to the glory of your Name. Amen.

Hail Mary

Hail Mary, full of grace. The Lord is with you. Blessed are you amongst women, and blessed is the fruit of your womb, Jesus. Holy Mary, Mother of God, pray for us sinners, now and at the hour of our death. Amen.

Closing Prayer

May God grant me a peaceful night and a perfect end. May the divine assistance be always with me and with all my loved ones.

Spiritual Journal

What have I done, what have I failed to do today? What have I said, what have I failed to say today? What could I do better?

Day Six: Morning Prayer

Please take a moment of silence and quiet time.

Opening Prayer

O God, open my lips, and my mouth will proclaim your praise.

Peace and Social Justice Quote

Christ our Lord did not come to bring peace to the world as a kind of spiritual tranquilizer. He brought to his disciples a vocation and a task – to struggle in the world of violence to establish his peace not only in their own hearts but in society itself.

—Thomas Merton

Prayer

Concerned God, help me to mirror your peace in my heart and as I strive to promote peace in society.

Please take a short period of time to contemplate the quote.

Canticle of Zechariah

Blessed are you, O God, for you have turned to your people and saved us and set us free. You have raised up for us a strong deliverer, and so you promised: age after age you proclaimed by the lips of your holy prophets that you would deliver us, calling to mind your solemn covenant. This was the promise that you made: to rescue us and free us from fear, so that we might worship you with a holy worship, in your holy presence our whole life long. In your tender compassion, the morning sun has risen upon us – to shine on us in our darkness, to guide our feet into the paths of peace.

Our Father

Our Father, who art in heaven, hallowed be your name; your kingdom come; your will be done on earth as it is in heaven. Give us this day our daily bread; and forgive us our trespasses as we forgive those who trespass against us; and lead us not into temptation, but deliver us from evil. Amen.

Closing Prayer

May God be gracious to me, show me kindness, and fill my heart with peace.

Spiritual Journal

My peace and social justice intent for today:

Day Six: Evening Prayer

Please take a moment of silence and quiet time.

Opening Prayer

God, come to my assistance. Holy One, make haste to help me.

Peace and Social Justice Quote

Christ our Lord did not come to bring peace to the world as a kind of spiritual tranquilizer. He brought to his disciples a vocation and a task – to struggle in the world of violence to establish his peace not only in their own hearts but in society itself.

—Thomas Merton

Prayer

Concerning God, help me to mirror your peace in my heart and as I strive to promote peace in society.

Please take a short period of time to contemplate the quote.

Canticle of Mary

Our souls proclaim the glory of the Holy One; our spirits rejoice in God, our Savior, for you have looked with favor upon your lowly servant. You have done great things and holy is your name. You have cast down the mighty, and lifted up the lowly; you have filled the hungry with good things, and have sent the rich away empty. You have come to your children and set them free, for you have

remembered your promise of mercy to our mothers and fathers, and to all your children forever.

Examination of Conscience

In what ways have I mirrored God and in what concrete ways have I promoted peace today? What could I do better?

Act of Contrition

Most merciful God, we confess that we have sinned against you in thought, word, and deed, by what we have done, and by what we have left undone. We have not loved you with our whole heart; we have not loved our neighbors as ourselves. We are truly sorry and we humbly repent. For the sake of your Son Jesus Christ, have mercy on us and forgive us; that we may delight in your will, and walk in your ways, to the glory of your Name. Amen.

Hail Mary

Hail Mary, full of grace. The Lord is with you. Blessed are you amongst women, and blessed is the fruit of your womb, Jesus. Holy Mary, Mother of God, pray for us sinners, now and at the hour of our death. Amen.

Closing Prayer

May God grant me a peaceful night and a perfect end. May the divine assistance be always with me and with all my loved ones.

Spiritual Journal

What have I done, what have I failed to do today? What have I said, what have I failed to say today? What could I do better?

Day Seven: Morning Prayer

Please take a moment of silence and quiet time.

Opening Prayer

O God, open my lips, and my mouth will proclaim your praise.

Peace and Social Justice Quote

While you are proclaiming peace with you lips, be careful to have it even more fully in your heart.

—St. Francis

Prayer

Gentle God, help me with my desire to have peace in my heart.

Please take a short period of time to contemplate the quote.

Canticle of Zechariah

Blessed are you, O God, for you have turned to your people and saved us and set us free. You have raised up for us a strong deliverer, and so you promised: age after age you proclaimed by the lips of your holy prophets that you would deliver us, calling to mind your solemn covenant. This was the promise that you made: to rescue us and free us from fear, so that we might worship you with a holy worship, in your holy presence our whole life long. In your tender compassion, the morning sun has risen upon us – to shine on us in our darkness, to guide our feet into the paths of peace.

Our Father

Our Father, who art in heaven, hallowed be your name; your kingdom come; your will be done on earth as it is in heaven. Give us this day our daily bread; and forgive us our trespasses as we forgive those who trespass against us; and lead us not into temptation, but deliver us from evil. Amen.

Closing Prayer

May God be gracious to me, show me kindness, and fill my heart with peace.

Spiritual Journal

My peace and social justice intent for today:

Day Seven: Evening Prayer

Please take a moment of silence and quiet time.

Opening Prayer

God, come to my assistance. Holy One, make haste to help me.

Peace and Social Justice Quote

While you are proclaiming peace with you lips, be careful to have it even more fully in your heart.

—St. Francis

Please take a short period of time to contemplate the quote.

Prayer

Gentle God, help me with my desire to have peace in my heart.

Canticle of Mary

Our souls proclaim the glory of the Holy One; our spirits rejoice in God, our Savior, for you have looked with favor upon your lowly servant. You have done great things and holy is your name. You have cast down the mighty, and lifted up the lowly; you have filled the hungry with good things, and have sent the rich away empty. You have come to your children and set them free, for you have remembered your promise of mercy to our mothers and fathers, and to all your children forever.

Examination of Conscience

Was there peace in my heart today? What could I do better?

Act of Contrition

Most merciful God, we confess that we have sinned against you in thought, word, and deed, by what we have done, and by what we have left undone. We have not loved you with our whole heart; we have not loved our neighbors as ourselves. We are truly sorry and we humbly repent. For the sake of your Son Jesus Christ, have mercy on us and forgive us; that we may delight in your will, and walk in your ways, to the glory of your Name. Amen.

Hail Mary

Hail Mary, full of grace. The Lord is with you. Blessed are you amongst women, and blessed is the fruit of your womb, Jesus. Holy Mary, Mother of God, pray for us sinners, now and at the hour of our death. Amen.

Closing Prayer

May God grant me a peaceful night and a perfect end. May the divine assistance be always with me and with all my loved ones.

Spiritual Journal

What have I done, what have I failed to do today? What have I said, what have I failed to say today? What could I do better?

Day Eight: Morning Prayer

Please take a moment of silence and quiet time.

Opening Prayer

O God, open my lips, and my mouth will proclaim your praise.

Peace and Social Justice Quote

It's a barren prayer that does not go hand in hand with alms.

—St. Cyprian

Prayer

Kindhearted God, render me with the compassion to work for social and economic justice among the poor and vulnerable.

Please take a short period of time to contemplate the quote.

Canticle of Zechariah

Blessed are you, O God, for you have turned to your people and saved us and set us free. You have raised up for us a strong deliverer, and so you promised: age after age you proclaimed by the lips of your holy prophets that you would deliver us, calling to mind your solemn covenant. This was the promise that you made: to rescue us and free us from fear, so that we might worship you with a holy worship, in your holy presence our whole life long. In your tender compassion, the morning sun has risen upon us – to shine on us in our darkness, to guide our feet into the paths of peace.

Our Father

Our Father, who art in heaven, hallowed be your name; your kingdom come; your will be done on earth as it is in heaven. Give us this day our daily bread; and forgive us our trespasses as we forgive those who trespass against us; and lead us not into temptation, but deliver us from evil. Amen.

Closing Prayer

May God be gracious to me, show me kindness, and fill my heart with peace.

Spiritual Journal

My peace and social justice intent for today:

Day Eight: Evening Prayer

Please take a moment of silence and quiet time.

Opening Prayer

God, come to my assistance. Holy One, make haste to help me.

Peace and Social Justice Quote

It's a barren prayer that does not go hand in hand with alms.

—St. Cyprian

Prayer

Kindhearted God, render me with the compassion to work for social and economic justice among the poor and vulnerable.

Please take a short period of time to contemplate the quote.

Canticle of Mary

Our souls proclaim the glory of the Holy One; our spirits rejoice in God, our Savior, for you have looked with favor upon your lowly servant. You have done great things and holy is your name. You have cast down the mighty, and lifted up the lowly; you have filled the hungry with good things, and have sent the rich away empty. You have come to your children and set them free, for you have remembered your promise of mercy to our mothers and fathers, and to all your children forever.

Examination of Conscience

In what ways did I work for social and economic justice for the poor and vulnerable today? What could I do better?

Act of Contrition

Most merciful God, we confess that we have sinned against you in thought, word, and deed, by what we have done, and by what we have left undone. We have not loved you with our whole heart; we have not loved our neighbors as ourselves. We are truly sorry and we humbly repent. For the sake of your Son Jesus Christ, have mercy on us and forgive us; that we may delight in your will, and walk in your ways, to the glory of your Name. Amen.

Hail Mary

Hail Mary, full of grace. The Lord is with you. Blessed are you amongst women, and blessed is the fruit of your womb, Jesus. Holy Mary, Mother of God, pray for us sinners, now and at the hour of our death. Amen.

Closing Prayer

May God grant me a peaceful night and a perfect end. May the divine assistance be always with me and with all my loved ones.

Spiritual Journal

What have I done, what have I failed to do today? What have I said, what have I failed to say today? What could I do better?

Day Nine: Morning Prayer

Please take a moment of silence and quiet time.

Opening Prayer

O God, open my lips, and my mouth will proclaim your praise.

Peace and Social Justice Quote

The most faithful disciples of Christ have been builders of peace, to the point of forgiving their enemies, sometimes even to the point of giving their lives.

—Saint John Paul II

Prayer

Holy God, aid me in forgiving my enemies.

Please take a short period of time to contemplate the quote.

Canticle of Zechariah

Blessed are you, O God, for you have turned to your people and saved us and set us free. You have raised up for us a strong deliverer, and so you promised: age after age you proclaimed by the lips of your holy prophets that you would deliver us, calling to mind your solemn covenant. This was the promise that you made: to rescue us and free us from fear, so that we might worship you with a holy worship, in your holy presence our whole life long. In your tender compassion, the morning sun has risen upon us —

to shine on us in our darkness, to guide our feet into the paths of peace.

Our Father

Our Father, who art in heaven, hallowed be your name; your kingdom come; your will be done on earth as it is in heaven. Give us this day our daily bread; and forgive us our trespasses as we forgive those who trespass against us; and lead us not into temptation, but deliver us from evil. Amen.

Closing Prayer

May God be gracious to me, show me kindness, and fill my heart with peace.

Spiritual Journal

My peace and social justice intent for today:

Day Nine: Evening Prayer

Please take a moment of silence and quiet time.

Opening Prayer

God, come to my assistance. Holy One, make haste to help me.

Peace and Social Justice Quote

The most faithful disciples of Christ have been builders of peace, to the point of forgiving their enemies, sometimes even to the point of giving their lives.

—Saint John Paul II

Prayer

Holy God, aid me in forgiving my enemies.

Please take a short period of time to contemplate the quote.

Canticle of Mary

Our souls proclaim the glory of the Holy One; our spirits rejoice in God, our Savior, for you have looked with favor upon your lowly servant. You have done great things and holy is your name. You have cast down the mighty, and lifted up the lowly; you have filled the hungry with good things, and have sent the rich away empty. You have come to your children and set them free, for you have remembered your promise of mercy to our mothers and fathers, and to all your children forever.

Examination of Conscience

What attempts did I make to make amends with my enemies today? What could I do better?

Act of Contrition

Most merciful God, we confess that we have sinned against you in thought, word, and deed, by what we have done, and by what we have left undone. We have not loved you with our whole heart; we have not loved our neighbors as ourselves. We are truly sorry and we humbly repent. For the sake of your Son Jesus Christ, have mercy on us and forgive us; that we may delight in your will, and walk in your ways, to the glory of your Name. Amen.

Hail Mary

Hail Mary, full of grace. The Lord is with you. Blessed are you amongst women, and blessed is the fruit of your womb, Jesus. Holy Mary, Mother of God, pray for us sinners, now and at the hour of our death. Amen.

Closing Prayer

May God grant me a peaceful night and a perfect end. May the divine assistance be always with me and with all my loved ones.

Spiritual Journal

What have I done, what have I failed to do today? What have I said, what have I failed to say today? What could I do better?

Day Ten: Morning Prayer

Please take a moment of silence and quiet time.

Opening Prayer

O God, open my lips, and my mouth will proclaim your praise.

Peace and Social Justice Quote

We who have a voice must speak for the voiceless.

—Archbishop Oscar Romero

Prayer

Tender God, assist me with your compassion and help me to be a voice for the voiceless.

Please take a short period of time to contemplate the quote.

Canticle of Zechariah

Blessed are you, O God, for you have turned to your people and saved us and set us free. You have raised up for us a strong deliverer, and so you promised: age after age you proclaimed by the lips of your holy prophets that you would deliver us, calling to mind your solemn covenant. This was the promise that you made: to rescue us and free us from fear, so that we might worship you with a holy worship, in your holy presence our whole life long. In your tender compassion, the morning sun has risen upon us – to shine on us in our darkness, to guide our feet into the paths of peace.

Our Father

Our Father, who art in heaven, hallowed be your name; your kingdom come; your will be done on earth as it is in heaven. Give us this day our daily bread; and forgive us our trespasses as we forgive those who trespass against us; and lead us not into temptation, but deliver us from evil. Amen.

Closing Prayer

May God be gracious to me, show me kindness, and fill my heart with peace.

Spiritual Journal

My peace and social justice intent for today:

Day Ten: Evening Prayer

Please take a moment of silence and quiet time.

Opening Prayer

God, come to my assistance. Holy One, make haste to help me.

Peace and Social Justice Quote

We who have a voice must speak for the voiceless.

—Archbishop Oscar Romero

Prayer

Tender God, assist me with your compassion and help me to be a voice for the voiceless.

Please take a short period of time to contemplate the quote.

Canticle of Mary

Our souls proclaim the glory of the Holy One; or spirits rejoice in God, our Savior, for you have looked with favor upon your lowly servant. You have done great things and holy is your name. You have cast down the mighty, and lifted up the lowly; you have filled the hungry with good things, and have sent the rich away empty. You have come to your children and set them free, for you have remembered your promise of mercy to our mothers and fathers, and to all your children forever.

Examination of Conscience

When did I speak on behalf of someone who did not have a voice today? What could I do better?

Act of Contrition

Most merciful God, we confess that we have sinned against you in thought, word, and deed, by what we have done, and by what we have left undone. We have not loved you with our whole heart; we have not loved our neighbors as ourselves. We are truly sorry and we humbly repent. For the sake of your Son Jesus Christ, have mercy on us and forgive us; that we may delight in your will, and walk in your ways, to the glory of your Name. Amen.

Hail Mary

Hail Mary, full of grace. The Lord is with you. Blessed art you amongst women, and blessed is the fruit of your womb, Jesus. Holy Mary, Mother of God, pray for us sinners, now and at the hour of our death. Amen.

Closing Prayer

May God grant me a peaceful night and a perfect end. May the divine assistance be always with me and with all my loved ones.

Spiritual Journal

What have I done, what have I failed to do today? What have I said, what have I failed to say today? What could I do better?

Day Eleven: Morning Prayer

Please take a moment of silence and quiet time.

Opening Prayer

O God, open my lips, and my mouth will proclaim your praise.

Peace and Social Justice Quote

To overcome today's individualistic mentality, a concrete commitment to solidarity and charity is needed, beginning in the family.

—Saint John Paul II

Prayer

Caring God, allow my commitment to charity begin with my family.

Please take a short period of time to contemplate the quote.

Canticle of Zechariah

Blessed are you, O God, for you have turned to your people and saved us and set us free. You have raised up for us a strong deliverer, and so you promised: age after age you proclaimed by the lips of your holy prophets that you would deliver us, calling to mind your solemn covenant. This was the promise that you made: to rescue us and free us from fear, so that we might worship you with a holy worship, in your holy presence our whole life long. In your tender compassion, the morning sun has risen upon us – to shine on us in our darkness, to guide our feet into the paths of peace.

Our Father

Our Father, who art in heaven, hallowed be your name; your kingdom come; your will be done on earth as it is in heaven. Give us this day our daily bread; and forgive us our trespasses as we forgive those who trespass against us; and lead us not into temptation, but deliver us from evil. Amen.

Closing Prayer

May God be gracious to me, show me kindness, and fill my heart with peace.

Spiritual Journal

My peace and social justice intent for today:

Day Eleven: Evening Prayer

Please take a moment of silence and quiet time.

Opening Prayer

God, come to my assistance. Holy One, make haste to help me.

Peace and Social Justice Quote

To overcome today's individualistic mentality, a concrete commitment to solidarity and charity is needed, beginning in the family.

—Saint John Paul II

Prayer

Caring God, allow my commitment to charity begin with my family.

Please take a short period of time to contemplate the quote.

Canticle of Mary

Our souls proclaim the glory of the Holy One; our spirits rejoice in God, our Savior, for you have looked with favor upon your lowly servant. You have done great things and holy is your name. You have cast down the mighty, and lifted up the lowly; you have filled the hungry with good things, and have sent the rich away empty. You have come to your children and set them free, for you have remembered your promise of mercy to our mothers and fathers, and to all your children forever.

Examination of Conscience

In what concrete ways have I been charitable with my family today? What could I do better?

Act of Contrition

Most merciful God, we confess that we have sinned against you in thought, word, and deed, by what we have done, and by what we have left undone. We have not loved you with our whole heart; we have not loved our neighbors as ourselves. We are truly sorry and we humbly repent. For the sake of your Son Jesus Christ, have mercy on us and forgive us; that we may delight in your will, and walk in your ways, to the glory of your Name. Amen.

Hail Mary

Hail Mary, full of grace. The Lord is with you. Blessed are you amongst women, and blessed is the fruit of your womb, Jesus. Holy Mary, Mother of God, pray for us sinners, now and at the hour of our death. Amen.

Closing Prayer

May God grant me a peaceful night and a perfect end. May the divine assistance be always with me and with all my loved ones.

Spiritual Journal

What have I done, what have I failed to do today? What have I said, what have I failed to say today? What could I do better?

Day Twelve: Morning Prayer

Please take a moment of silence and quiet time.

Opening Prayer

O God, open my lips, and my mouth will proclaim your praise.

Peace and Social Justice Quote

What can you do to promote world peace? Go home and love your family.

—St. Teresa of India

Please take a short period of time to contemplate the quote.

Prayer

Peaceful God, render me the disposition to promote peace and love in my family.

Canticle of Zechariah

Blessed are you, O God, for you have turned to your people and saved us and set us free. You have raised up for us a strong deliverer, and so you promised: age after age you proclaimed by the lips of your holy prophets that you would deliver us, calling to mind your solemn covenant. This was the promise that you made: to rescue us and free us from fear, so that we might worship you with a holy worship, in your holy presence our whole life long. In your

tender compassion, the morning sun has risen upon us – to shine on us in our darkness, to guide our feet into the paths of peace.

Our Father

Our Father, who art in heaven, hallowed be your name; your kingdom come; your will be done on earth as it is in heaven. Give us this day our daily bread; and forgive us our trespasses as we forgive those who trespass against us; and lead us not into temptation, but deliver us from evil. Amen.

Closing Prayer

May God be gracious to me, show me kindness, and fill my heart with peace.

Spiritual Journal

My peace and social justice intent for today:

Day Twelve: Evening Prayer

Please take a moment of silence and quiet time.

Opening Prayer

God, come to my assistance. Holy One, make haste to help me.

Peace and Social Justice Quote

What can you do to promote world peace? Go home and love your family.

—St. Teresa

Prayer

Peaceful God, render me the disposition to promote peace and love in my family.

Please take a short period of time to contemplate the quote.

Canticle of Mary

Our souls proclaim the glory of the Holy One; our spirits rejoice in God, our Savior, for you have looked with favor upon your lowly servant. You have done great things and holy is your name. You have cast down the mighty, and lifted up the lowly; you have filled the hungry with good things, and have sent the rich away empty. You have come to your children and set them free, for you have remembered your promise of mercy to our mothers and fathers, and to all your children forever.

Examination of Conscience

Did my disposition further peace and love in my family today? What could I do better?

Act of Contrition

Most merciful God, we confess that we have sinned against you in thought, word, and deed, by what we have done, and by what we have left undone. We have not loved you with our whole heart; we have not loved our neighbors as ourselves. We are truly sorry and we humbly repent. For the sake of your Son Jesus Christ, have mercy on us and forgive us; that we may delight in your will, and walk in your ways, to the glory of your Name. Amen.

Hail Mary

Hail Mary, full of grace. The Lord is with you. Blessed are you amongst women, and blessed is the fruit of your womb, Jesus. Holy Mary, Mother of God, pray for us sinners, now and at the hour of our death. Amen.

Closing Prayer

May God grant me a peaceful night and a perfect end. May the divine assistance be always with me and with all my loved ones.

Spiritual Journal

What have I done, what have I failed to do today? What have I said, what have I failed to say today? What could I do better?

Day Thirteen: Morning Prayer

Please take a moment of silence and quiet time.

Opening Prayer

O God, open my lips, and my mouth will proclaim your praise.

Peace and Social Justice Quote

The fullness of joy is to behold God in everything.

—Julian of Norwich

Prayer

Joyful God, help me to discover delight in all of your creation.

Please take a short period of time to contemplate the quote.

Canticle of Zechariah

Blessed are you, O God, for you have turned to your people and saved us and set us free. You have raised up for us a strong deliverer, and so you promised: age after age you proclaimed by the lips of your holy prophets that you would deliver us, calling to mind your solemn covenant. This was the promise that you made: to rescue us and free us from fear, so that we might worship you with a holy worship, in your holy presence our whole life long. In your tender compassion, the morning sun has risen upon us – to shine on us in our darkness, to guide our feet into the paths of peace.

Our Father

Our Father, who art in heaven, hallowed be your name; your kingdom come; your will be done on earth as it is in heaven. Give us this day our daily bread; and forgive us our trespasses as we forgive those who trespass against us; and lead us not into temptation, but deliver us from evil. Amen.

Closing Prayer

May God be gracious to me, show me kindness, and fill my heart with peace.

Spiritual Journal

My peace and social justice intent for today:

Day Thirteen: Evening Prayer

Please take a moment of silence and quiet time.

Opening Prayer

God, come to my assistance. Holy One, make haste to help me.

Peace and Social Justice Quote

The fullness of joy is to behold God in everything.

—Julian of Norwich

Prayer

Joyful God, help me to discover delight in all of your creation.

Please take a short period of time to contemplate the quote.

Canticle of Mary

Our souls proclaim the glory of the Holy One; our spirits rejoice in God, our Savior, for you have looked with favor upon your lowly servant. You have done great things and holy is your name. You have cast down the mighty, and lifted up the lowly; you have filled the hungry with good things, and have sent the rich away empty. You have come to your children and set them free, for you have remembered your promise of mercy to our mothers and fathers, and to all your children forever.

Examination of Conscience

To what extent did I consider God in everything today? What could I do better?

Act of Contrition

Most merciful God, we confess that we have sinned against you in thought, word, and deed, by what we have done, and by what we have left undone. We have not loved you with our whole heart; we have not loved our neighbors as ourselves. We are truly sorry and we humbly repent. For the sake of your Son Jesus Christ, have mercy on us and forgive us; that we may delight in your will, and walk in your ways, to the glory of your Name. Amen.

Hail Mary

Hail Mary, full of grace. The Lord is with you. Blessed are you amongst women, and blessed is the fruit of your womb, Jesus. Holy Mary, Mother of God, pray for us sinners, now and at the hour of our death. Amen.

Closing Prayer

May God grant me a peaceful night and a perfect end. May the divine assistance be always with me and with all my loved ones.

Spiritual Journal

What have I done, what have I failed to do today? What have I said, what have I failed to say today? What could I do better?

Day Fourteen: Morning Prayer

Please take a moment of silence and quiet time.

Opening Prayer

O God, open my lips, and my mouth will proclaim your praise.

Peace and Social Justice Quote

We Christians do not bear arms against any country; we do not make war anymore. We have become children of peace; Jesus is our leader.

—Origin 3rd Century.

Prayer

Nonviolent God, guide me to the gentle spiritual values of Jesus.

Please take a short period of time to contemplate the quote.

Canticle of Zechariah

Blessed are you, O God, for you have turned to your people and saved us and set us free. You have raised up for us a strong deliverer, and so you promised: age after age you proclaimed by the lips of your holy prophets that you would deliver us, calling to mind your solemn covenant. This was the promise that you made: to rescue us and free us from fear, so that we might worship you with a holy worship, in your holy presence our whole life long. In your tender compassion, the morning sun has risen upon us – to shine on us in our darkness, to guide our feet into the paths of peace.

Our Father

Our Father, who art in heaven, hallowed be your name; your king-dom come; your will be done on earth as it is in heaven. Give us this day our daily bread; and forgive us our trespasses as we forgive those who trespass against us; and lead us not into temptation, but deliver us from evil. Amen.

Closing Prayer

May God be gracious to me, show me kindness, and fill my heart with peace.

Spiritual Journal

My peace and social justice intent for today:

Day Fourteen: Evening Prayer

Please take a moment of silence and quiet time.

Opening Prayer

God, come to my assistance. Holy One, make haste to help me.

Peace and Social Justice Quote

We Christians do not bear arms against any country; we do not make war anymore. We have become children of peace; Jesus is our leader.

—Origin 3rd Century.

Prayer

Nonviolent God, guide me to the gentle spiritual values of Jesus.

Please take a short period of time to contemplate the quote.

Canticle of Mary

Our souls proclaim the glory of the Holy One; our spirits rejoice in God, our Savior, for you have looked with favor upon your lowly servant. You have done great things and holy is your name. You have cast down the mighty, and lifted up the lowly; you have filled the hungry with good things, and have sent the rich away empty. You have come to your children and set them free, for you have remembered your promise of mercy to our mothers and fathers, and to all your children forever.

Examination of Conscience

Was I a child of peace as a follower of Jesus today? What could I do better?

Act of Contrition

Most merciful God, we confess that we have sinned against you in thought, word, and deed, by what we have done, and by what we have left undone. We have not loved you with our whole heart; we have not loved our neighbors as ourselves. We are truly sorry and we humbly repent. For the sake of your Son Jesus Christ, have mercy on us and forgive us; that we may delight in your will, and walk in your ways, to the glory of your Name. Amen.

Hail Mary

Hail Mary, full of grace. The Lord is with you. Blessed are you amongst women, and blessed is the fruit of your womb, Jesus. Holy Mary, Mother of God, pray for us sinners, now and at the hour of our death. Amen.

Closing Prayer

May God grant me a peaceful night and a perfect end. May the divine assistance be always with me and with all my loved ones.

Spiritual Journal

What have I done, what have I failed to do today? What have I said, what have I failed to say today? What could I do better?

Day Fifteen: Morning Prayer

Please take a moment of silence and quiet time.

Opening Prayer

O God, open my lips, and my mouth will proclaim your praise.

Peace and Social Justice Quote

Much violence is based on the illusion that life is a property to be defended and not a gift to be shared.

—Henri Nouwen

Prayer

Incarnate God, help me to recognize the needs of my neighbor and share what I have as an expression of your truth and a way to foster nonviolence in this world today.

Please take a short period of time to contemplate the quote.

Canticle of Zechariah

Blessed are you, O God, for you have turned to your people and saved us and set us free. You have raised up for us a strong deliverer, and so you promised: age after age you proclaimed by the lips of your holy prophets that you would deliver us, calling to mind your solemn covenant. This was the promise that you made: to rescue us and free us from fear, so that we might worship you with a holy worship, in your holy presence our whole life long. In your

tender compassion, the morning sun has risen upon us – to shine on us in our darkness, to guide our feet into the paths of peace.

Our Father

Our Father, who art in heaven, hallowed be your name; your kingdom come; your will be done on earth as it is in heaven. Give us this day our daily bread; and forgive us our trespasses as we forgive those who trespass against us; and lead us not into temptation, but deliver us from evil. Amen.

Closing Prayer

May God be gracious to me, show me kindness, and fill my heart with peace.

Spiritual Journal

My peace and social justice intent for today:

Day Fifteen: Evening Prayer

Please take a moment of silence and quiet time.

Opening Prayer

God, come to my assistance. Holy One, make haste to help me.

Peace and Social Justice Quote

Much violence is based on the illusion that life is a property to be defended and not a gift to be shared.

—Henri Nouwen

Prayer

Incarnate God, help me to recognize the needs of my neighbor and share what I have as an expression of your truth and a way to foster nonviolence in this world.

Please take a short period of time to contemplate the quote.

Canticle of Mary

Our souls proclaim the glory of the Holy One; our spirits rejoice in God, our Savior, for you have looked with favor upon your lowly servant. You have done great things and holy is your name. You have cast down the mighty, and lifted up the lowly; you have filled the hungry with good things, and have sent the rich away empty. You have come to your children and set them free, for you have

remembered your promise of mercy to our mothers and fathers, and to all your children forever.

Examination of Conscience

In what ways did I share what I have with my neighbor today? What could I do better?

Act of Contrition

Most merciful God, we confess that we have sinned against you in thought, word, and deed, by what we have done, and by what we have left undone. We have not loved you with our whole heart; we have not loved our neighbors as ourselves. We are truly sorry and we humbly repent. For the sake of your Son Jesus Christ, have mercy on us and forgive us; that we may delight in your will, and walk in your ways, to the glory of your Name. Amen.

Hail Mary

Hail Mary, full of grace. The Lord is with you. Blessed are you amongst women, and blessed is the fruit of your womb, Jesus. Holy Mary, Mother of God, pray for us sinners, now and at the hour of our death. Amen.

Closing Prayer

May God grant me a peaceful night and a perfect end. May the divine assistance be always with me and with all my loved ones.

Spiritual Journal

What have I done, what have I failed to do today? What have I said, what have I failed to say today? What could I do better?

Day Sixteen: Morning Prayer

Please take a moment of silence and quiet time.

Opening Prayer

O God, open my lips, and my mouth will proclaim your praise.

Peace and Social Justice Quote

If murder is committed privately it is considered a crime. But if it happens with the authority of the state, they call it courage.

—St. Cyprian

Prayer

Teaching God, inspire me to strive for an end to capital punishment.

Please take a short period of time to contemplate the quote.

Canticle of Zechariah

Blessed are you, O God, for you have turned to your people and saved us and set us free. You have raised up for us a strong deliverer, and so you promised: age after age you proclaimed by the lips of your holy prophets that you would deliver us, calling to mind your solemn covenant. This was the promise that you made: to rescue us and free us from fear, so that we might worship you with a holy worship, in your holy presence our whole life long. In your tender compassion, the morning sun has risen upon us –

to shine on us in our darkness, to guide our feet into the paths of peace.

Our Father

Our Father, who art in heaven, hallowed be your name; your kingdom come; your will be done on earth as it is in heaven. Give us this day our daily bread; and forgive us our trespasses as we forgive those who trespass against us; and lead us not into temptation, but deliver us from evil. Amen.

Closing Prayer

May God be gracious to me, show me kindness, and fill my heart with peace.

Spiritual Journal

My peace and social justice intent for today:

Day Sixteen: Evening Prayer

Please take a moment of silence and quiet time.

Opening Prayer

God, come to my assistance. Holy One, make haste to help me.

Peace and Social Justice Quote

If murder is committed privately it is considered a crime. But if it happens with the authority of the state, they call it courage.

—St. Cyprian

Prayer

Teaching God, inspire me to strive for an end to capital punishment.

Please take a short period of time to contemplate the quote.

Canticle of Mary

Our souls proclaim the glory of the Holy One; our spirits rejoice in God, our Savior, for you have looked with favor upon your lowly servant. You have done great things and holy is your name. You have cast down the mighty, and lifted up the lowly; you have filled the hungry with good things, and have sent the rich away empty. You have come to your children and set them free, for you have remembered your promise of mercy to our mothers and fathers, and to all your children forever.

Examination of Conscience

What efforts have I made to end capital punishment today? What could I do better?

Act of Contrition

Most merciful God, we confess that we have sinned against you in thought, word, and deed, by what we have done, and by what we have left undone. We have not loved you with our whole heart; we have not loved our neighbors as ourselves. We are truly sorry and we humbly repent. For the sake of your Son Jesus Christ, have mercy on us and forgive us; that we may delight in your will, and walk in your ways, to the glory of your Name. Amen.

Hail Mary

Hail Mary, full of grace. The Lord is with you. Blessed are you amongst women, and blessed is the fruit of your womb, Jesus. Holy Mary, Mother of God, pray for us sinners, now and at the hour of our death. Amen.

Closing Prayer

May God grant me a peaceful night and a perfect end. May the divine assistance be always with me and with all my loved ones.

Spiritual Journal

What have I done, what have I failed to do today? What have I said, what have I failed to say today? What could I do better?

Day Seventeen: Morning Prayer

Please take a moment of silence and quiet time.

Opening Prayer

O God, open my lips, and my mouth will proclaim your praise.

Peace and Social Justice Quote

When a poor person dies of hunger, it has not happened because God did not take care of him or her. It has happened because neither you nor I wanted to give that person what he or she needed.

—St. Teresa

Please take a short period of time to contemplate the quote.

Canticle of Zechariah

Blessed are you, O God, for you have turned to your people and saved us and set us free. You have raised up for us a strong deliverer, and so you promised: age after age you proclaimed by the lips of your holy prophets that you would deliver us, calling to mind your solemn covenant. This was the promise that you made: to rescue us and free us from fear, so that we might worship you with a holy worship, in your holy presence our whole life long. In your tender compassion, the morning sun has risen upon us – to shine on us in our darkness, to guide our feet into the paths of peace.

Prayer

Challenging God, in the midst of hunger, homelessness, insecurity, and injustice, help me to help those in need today.

Our Father

Our Father, who art in heaven, hallowed be your name; your kingdom come; your will be done on earth as it is in heaven. Give us this day our daily bread; and forgive us our trespasses as we forgive those who trespass against us; and lead us not into temptation, but deliver us from evil. Amen.

Closing Prayer

May God be gracious to me, show me kindness, and fill my heart with peace.

Spiritual Journal

My peace and social justice intent for today:

Day Seventeen: Evening Prayer

Please take a moment of silence and quiet time.

Opening Prayer

God, come to my assistance. Holy One, make haste to help me.

Peace and Social Justice Quote

When a poor person dies of hunger, it has not happened because God did not take care of him or her. It has happened because neither you nor I wanted to give that person what he or she needed.

—St. Teresa

Prayer

Challenging God, in the midst of hunger, homelessness, insecurity, and injustice, help me to help those in need today.

Please take a short period of time to contemplate the quote.

Canticle of Mary

Our souls proclaim the glory of the Holy One; our spirits rejoice in God, our Savior, for you have looked with favor upon your lowly servant. You have done great things and holy is your name. you have cast down the mighty, and lifted up the lowly; you have filled the hungry with good things, and have sent the rich away empty. You have come to your children and set them free, for you have

remembered your promise of mercy to our mothers and fathers, and to all your children forever.

Examination of Conscience

Did I comfort when others are hungry, homeless, insecure today? What could I do better?

Act of Contrition

Most merciful God, we confess that we have sinned against you in thought, word, and deed, by what we have done, and by what we have left undone. We have not loved you with our whole heart; we have not loved our neighbors as ourselves. We are truly sorry and we humbly repent. For the sake of your Son Jesus Christ, have mercy on us and forgive us; that we may delight in your will, and walk in your ways, to the glory of your Name. Amen.

Hail Mary

Hail Mary, full of grace. The Lord is with you. Blessed are you amongst women, and blessed is the fruit of your womb, Jesus. Holy Mary, Mother of God, pray for us sinners, now and at the hour of our death. Amen.

Closing Prayer

May God grant me a peaceful night and a perfect end. May the divine assistance be always with me and with all my loved ones.

Spiritual Journal

What have I done, what have I failed to do today? What have I said, what have I failed to say today? What could I do better?

Day Eighteen: Morning Prayer

Please take a moment of silence and quiet time.

Opening Prayer

O God, open my lips, and my mouth will proclaim your praise.

Peace and Social Justice Quote

It is certainly a greater and more wonderful work to change the minds of enemies, bringing about a change of soul, than to kill them.

—St. John Chrysostom

Prayer

Inviting God, as I seek justice and pursue peace, sustain me as I seek reconciliation with those I consider my enemy so that I may mirror Jesus in the ways of charity and peace.

Please take a short period of time to contemplate the quote.

Canticle of Zechariah

Blessed are you, O God, for you have turned to your people and saved us and set us free. You have raised up for us a strong deliverer, and so you promised: age after age you proclaimed by the lips of your holy prophets that you would deliver us, calling to mind your solemn covenant. This was the promise that you made: to rescue us and free us from fear, so that we might worship you with a holy worship, in your holy presence our whole life long. In your tender compassion, the morning sun has risen upon us – to shine on us in our darkness, to guide our feet into the paths of peace.

Our Father

Our Father, who art in heaven, hallowed be your name; your kingdom come; your will be done on earth as it is in heaven. Give us this day our daily bread; and forgive us our trespasses as we forgive those who trespass against us; and lead us not into temptation, but deliver us from evil. Amen.

Closing Prayer

May God be gracious to me, show me kindness, and fill my heart with peace.

Spiritual Journal

My peace and social justice intent for today:

Day Eighteen: Evening Prayer

Please take a moment of silence and quiet time.

Opening Prayer

God, come to my assistance. Holy One, make haste to help me.

Peace and Social Justice Quote

It is certainly a greater and more wonderful work to change the minds of enemies, bringing about a change of soul, than to kill them.

—St. John Chrysostom

Prayer

Inviting God, as I seek justice and pursue peace, sustain me as I seek reconciliation with those I consider my enemy so that I may mirror Jesus in the ways of charity and peace.

Please take a short period of time to contemplate the quote.

Canticle of Mary

Our souls proclaim the glory of the Holy One; our spirits rejoice in God, our Savior, for you have looked with favor upon your lowly servant. You have done great things and holy is your name. You have cast down the mighty, and lifted up the lowly; you have filled the hungry with good things, and have sent the rich away empty. You have come to your children and set them free, for you have remembered your promise of mercy to our mothers and fathers, and to all your children forever.

Examination of Conscience

How have I sought justice, peace, and reconciliation with those I consider my enemy, rival and adversary today? What could I do better?

Act of Contrition

Most merciful God, we confess that we have sinned against you in thought, word, and deed, by what we have done, and by what we have left undone. We have not loved you with our whole heart; we have not loved our neighbors as ourselves. We are truly sorry and we humbly repent. For the sake of your Son Jesus Christ, have mercy on us and forgive us; that we may delight in your will, and walk in your ways, to the glory of your Name. Amen.

Hail Mary

Hail Mary, full of grace. The Lord is with you. Blessed are you amongst women, and blessed is the fruit of your womb, Jesus. Holy Mary, Mother of God, pray for us sinners, now and at the hour of our death. Amen.

Closing Prayer

May God grant me a peaceful night and a perfect end. May the divine assistance be always with me and with all my loved ones.

Spiritual Journal

What have I done, what have I failed to do today? What have I said, what have I failed to say today? What could I do better?

Day Nineteen: Morning Prayer

Opening Prayer

O God, open my lips, and my mouth will proclaim your praise.

Peace and Social Justice Quote

Everything a baptized person does each day should be directly or indirectly related to the corporal and spiritual works of mercy.

—Dorothy Day

Prayer

Gracious God, encourage me daily to provide corporal and spiritual works of mercy.

Please take a short period of time to contemplate the quote.

Canticle of Zechariah

Blessed are you, O God, for you have turned to your people and saved us and set us free. You have raised up for us a strong deliverer, and so you promised: age after age you proclaimed by the lips of your holy prophets that you would deliver us, calling to mind your solemn covenant. This was the promise that you made: to rescue us and free us from fear, so that we might worship you with a holy worship, in your holy presence our whole life long. In your tender compassion, the morning sun has risen upon us – to shine on us in our darkness, to guide our feet into the paths of peace.

Our Father

Our Father, who art in heaven, hallowed be your name; your kingdom come; your will be done on earth as it is in heaven. Give us this day our daily bread; and forgive us our trespasses as we forgive those who trespass against us; and lead us not into temptation, but deliver us from evil. Amen.

Closing Prayer

May God be gracious to me, show me kindness, and fill my heart with peace.

Spiritual Journal

My peace and social justice intent for today:

Day Nineteen: Evening Prayer

Please take a moment of silence and quiet time.

Opening Prayer

God, come to my assistance. Holy One, make haste to help me.

Peace and Social Justice Quote

Everything a baptized person does each day should be directly or indirectly related to the corporal and spiritual works of mercy.

—Dorothy Day

Prayer

Gracious God, encourage me daily to provide corporal and spiritual works of mercy.

Please take a short period of time to contemplate the quote.

Canticle of Mary

Our souls proclaim the glory of the Holy One; our spirits rejoice in God, our Savior, for you have looked with favor upon your lowly servant. You have done great things and holy is your name. You have cast down the mighty, and lifted up the lowly; you have filled the hungry with good things, and have sent the rich away empty. You have come to your children and set them free, for you have remembered your promise of mercy to our mothers and fathers, and to all your children forever.

Examination of Conscience

What works of corporal and spiritual works of mercy have I practiced today? What could I do better?

Act of Contrition

Most merciful God, we confess that we have sinned against you in thought, word, and deed, by what we have done, and by what we have left undone. We have not loved you with our whole heart; we have not loved our neighbors as ourselves. We are truly sorry and we humbly repent. For the sake of your Son Jesus Christ, have mercy on us and forgive us; that we may delight in your will, and walk in your ways, to the glory of your Name. Amen.

Hail Mary

Hail Mary, full of grace. The Lord is with you. Blessed are you amongst women, and blessed is the fruit of your womb, Jesus. Holy Mary, Mother of God, pray for us sinners, now and at the hour of our death. Amen.

Closing Prayer

May God grant me a peaceful night and a perfect end. May the divine assistance be always with me and with all my loved ones.

Spiritual Journal

What have I done, what have I failed to do today? What have I said, what have I failed to say today? What could I do better?

Day Twenty: Morning Prayer

Please take a moment of silence and quiet time.

Opening Prayer

O God, open my lips, and my mouth will proclaim your praise.

Peace and Social Justice Quote

If a person is gay and seeks God and has good will, who am I to judge?

—Pope Francis

Prayer

Gracious God, help me to be less judgmental toward gay people because of who they are and who they love.

Please take a short period of time to contemplate the quote.

Canticle of Zechariah

Blessed are you, O God, for you have turned to your people and saved us and set us free.You have raised up for us a strong deliverer, and so you promised: age after age you proclaimed by the lips of your holy prophets that you would deliver us, calling to mind your solemn covenant. This was the promise that you made: to rescue us and free us from fear, so that we might worship you with a holy worship, in your holy presence our whole life long. In your

tender compassion, the morning sun has risen upon us – to shine on us in our darkness, to guide our feet into the paths of peace.

Our Father

Our Father, who art in heaven, hallowed be your name; your kingdom come; your will be done on earth as it is in heaven. Give us this day our daily bread; and forgive us our trespasses as we forgive those who trespass against us; and lead us not into temptation, but deliver us from evil. Amen.

Closing Prayer

May God be gracious to me, show me kindness, and fill my heart with peace.

Spiritual Journal

My peace and social justice intent for today:

Day Twenty: Evening Prayer

Please take a moment of silence and quiet time.

Opening Prayer

God, come to my assistance. Holy One, make haste to help me.

Peace and Social Justice Quote

If a person is gay and seeks God and has good will, who am I to judge?

—Pope Francis

Prayer

Gracious God, help me to be less judgmental toward gay people because of who they are and who they love.

Please take a short period of time to contemplate the quote.

Canticle of Mary

Our souls proclaim the glory of the Holy One; our spirits rejoice in God, our Savior, for you have looked with favor upon your lowly servant. You have done great things and holy is your name. You have cast down the mighty, and lifted up the lowly; you have filled the hungry with good things, and have sent the rich away empty. You have come to your children and set them free, for you have remembered your promise of mercy to our mothers and fathers, and to all your children forever.

Examination of Conscience

Did I judge someone because of his or her sexual orientation today? What could I do better?

Act of Contrition

Most merciful God, we confess that we have sinned against you in thought, word, and deed, by what we have done, and by what we have left undone. We have not loved you with our whole heart; we have not loved our neighbors as ourselves. We are truly sorry and we humbly repent. For the sake of your Son Jesus Christ, have mercy on us and forgive us; that we may delight in your will, and walk in your ways, to the glory of your Name. Amen.

Hail Mary

Hail Mary, full of grace. The Lord is with you. Blessed are you amongst women, and blessed is the fruit of your womb, Jesus. Holy Mary, Mother of God, pray for us sinners, now and at the hour of our death. Amen.

Closing Prayer

May God grant me a peaceful night and a perfect end. May the divine assistance be always with me and with all my loved ones.

Spiritual Journal

What have I done, what have I failed to do today? What have I said, what have I failed to say today? What could I do better?

Day Twenty-One: Morning Prayer

Please take a moment of silence and quiet time.

Opening Prayer

O God, open my lips, and my mouth will proclaim your praise.

Peace and Social Justice Quote

We have a nation of go-getters. I want a nation of go-givers.

— Peter Maurin

Prayer

Giving God, enable me to be less self-serving and more self-giving.

Please take a short period of time to contemplate the quote.

Canticle of Zechariah

Blessed are you, O God, for you have turned to your people and saved us and set us free. You have raised up for us a strong deliverer, and so you promised: age after age you proclaimed by the lips of your holy prophets that you would deliver us, calling to mind your solemn covenant. This was the promise that you made: to rescue us and free us from fear, so that we might worship you with a holy worship, in your holy presence our whole life long. In Your tender compassion, the morning sun has risen upon us – to shine on us in our darkness, to guide our feet into the paths of peace.

Our Father

Our Father, who art in heaven, hallowed be your name; your kingdom come; your will be done on earth as it is in heaven. Give us this day our daily bread; and forgive us our trespasses as we forgive those who trespass against us; and lead us not into temptation, but deliver us from evil. Amen.

Closing Prayer

May God be gracious to me, show me kindness, and fill my heart with peace.

Spiritual Journal

My peace and social justice intent for today:

Day Twenty-One: Evening Prayer

Please take a moment of silence and quiet time.

Opening Prayer

God, come to my assistance. Holy One, make haste to help me.

Peace and Social Justice Quote

We have a nation of go-getters. I want a nation of go-givers.

— Peter Maurin

Prayer

Giving God, enable me to be less self-serving and more self-giving.

Please take a short period of time to contemplate the quote.

Canticle of Mary

Our souls proclaim the glory of the Holy One; our spirits rejoice in God, our Savior, for you have looked with favor upon your lowly servant. You have done great things and holy is your name. You have cast down the mighty, and lifted up the lowly; you have filled the hungry with good things, and have sent the rich away empty. You have come to your children and set them free, for you have remembered your promise of mercy to our mothers and fathers, and to all your children forever.

Examination of Conscience

Was I self-serving or self-giving with my family, at job, or in my community today? What could I do better?

Act of Contrition

Most merciful God, we confess that we have sinned against you in thought, word, and deed, by what we have done, and by what we have left undone. We have not loved you with our whole heart; we have not loved our neighbors as ourselves. We are truly sorry and we humbly repent. For the sake of your Son Jesus Christ, have mercy on us and forgive us; that we may delight in your will, and walk in your ways, to the glory of your Name. Amen.

Hail Mary

Hail Mary, full of grace. The Lord is with you. Blessed are you amongst women, and blessed is the fruit of your womb, Jesus. Holy Mary, Mother of God, pray for us sinners, now and at the hour of our death. Amen.

Closing Prayer

May God grant me a peaceful night and a perfect end. May the divine assistance be always with me and with all my loved ones.

Spiritual Journal

What have I done, what have I failed to do today? What have I said, what have I failed to say today? What could I do better?

Day Twenty-Two: Morning Prayer

Please take a moment of silence and quiet time.

Opening Prayer

O God, open my lips, and my mouth will proclaim your praise.

Peace and Social Justice Quote

God's love comforts the afflicted and afflicts the comfortable.

—Dorothy Day

Prayer

Inspiring God, if I am troubled, console me. If I am content, disturb my complacency.

Please take a short period of time to contemplate the quote.

Canticle of Zechariah

Blessed are you, O God, for you have turned to your people and saved us and set us free. You have raised up for us a strong deliverer, and so you promised: age after age you proclaimed by the lips of your holy prophets that you would deliver us, calling to mind your solemn covenant. This was the promise that you made: to rescue us and free us from fear, so that we might worship you with a holy worship, in your holy presence our whole life long. In your tender compassion, the morning sun has risen upon us – to shine on us in our darkness, to guide our feet into the paths of peace.

Our Father

Our Father, who art in heaven, hallowed be your name; your kingdom come; your will be done on earth as it is in heaven. Give us this day our daily bread; and forgive us our trespasses as we forgive those who trespass against us; and lead us not into temptation, but deliver us from evil. Amen.

Closing Prayer

May God be gracious to me, show me kindness, and fill my heart with peace.

Spiritual Journal

My peace and social justice intent for today:

Day Twenty-Two: Evening Prayer

Please take a moment of silence and quiet time.

Opening Prayer

God, come to my assistance. Holy One, make haste to help me.

Peace and Social Justice Quote

God's love comforts the afflicted and afflicts the comfortable.

—Dorothy Day

Prayer

Inspiring God, if I am troubled, console me. If I am content, disturb my complacency.

Please take a short period of time to contemplate the quote.

Canticle of Mary

Our souls proclaim the glory of the Holy One; our spirits rejoice in God, our Savior, for you have looked with favor upon your lowly servant. You have done great things and holy is your name. You have cast down the mighty, and lifted up the lowly; you have filled the hungry with good things, and have sent the rich away empty. you have come to your children and set them free, for you have remembered your promise of mercy to our mothers and fathers, and to all your children forever.

Examination of Conscience

Did I trust God to sustain me through my troubles and/or allow God to disturb my sanctimoniousness sense of self today? What could I do better?

Act of Contrition

Most merciful God, we confess that we have sinned against you in thought, word, and deed, by what we have done, and by what we have left undone. We have not loved you with our whole heart; we have not loved our neighbors as ourselves. We are truly sorry and we humbly repent. For the sake of your Son Jesus Christ, have mercy on us and forgive us; that we may delight in your will, and walk in your ways, to the glory of your Name. Amen.

Hail Mary

Hail Mary, full of grace. The Lord is with you. Blessed are you amongst women, and blessed is the fruit of your womb, Jesus. Holy Mary, Mother of God, pray for us sinners, now and at the hour of our death. Amen.

Closing Prayer

May God grant me a peaceful night and a perfect end. May the divine assistance be always with me and with all my loved ones.

Spiritual Journal

What have I done, what have I failed to do today? What have I said, what have I failed to say today? What could I do better?

Day Twenty-Three: Morning Prayer

Please take a moment of silence and quiet time.

Opening Prayer

O God, open my lips, and my mouth will proclaim your praise.

Peace and Social Justice Quote

If you can't feed 100 people, then feed just one.

—St. Teresa

Prayer

Reigning God, grace me with the virtue to feed at least one person is hungry today.

Please take a short period of time to contemplate the quote.

Canticle of Zechariah

Blessed are you, O God, for you have turned to your people and saved us and set us free. You have raised up for us a strong deliverer, and so you promised: age after age you proclaimed by the lips of your holy prophets that you would deliver us, calling to mind your solemn covenant. This was the promise that you made: to rescue us and free us from fear, so that we might worship you with a holy worship, in your holy presence our whole life long. In your tender compassion, the morning sun has risen upon us – to shine on us in our darkness, to guide our feet into the paths of peace.

Our Father

Our Father, who art in heaven, hallowed be your name; your kingdom come; your will be done on earth as it is in heaven. Give us this day our daily bread; and forgive us our trespasses as we forgive those who trespass against us; and lead us not into temptation, but deliver us from evil. Amen.

Closing Prayer

May God be gracious to me, show me kindness, and fill my heart with peace.

Spiritual Journal

My peace and social justice intent for today:

Day Twenty-Three: Evening Prayer

Please take a moment of silence and quiet time.

Opening Prayer

God, come to my assistance. Holy One, make haste to help me.

Peace and Social Justice Quote

If you can't feed 100 people, then feed just one.

—St. Teresa

Prayer

Reigning God, grace me with the virtue to feed at least one person who is hungry.

Please take a short period of time to contemplate the quote.

Canticle of Mary

Our souls proclaim the glory of the Holy One; our spirits rejoice in God, our Savior, for you have looked with favor upon your lowly servant. You have done great things and holy is your name. You have cast down the mighty, and lifted up the lowly; you have filled the hungry with good things, and have sent the rich away empty. You have come to your children and set them free, for you have remembered your promise of mercy to our mothers and fathers, and to all your children forever.

Examination of Conscience

Who did I feed today? What could I do better?

Act of Contrition

Most merciful God, we confess that we have sinned against you in thought, word, and deed, by what we have done, and by what we have left undone. We have not loved you with our whole heart; we have not loved our neighbors as ourselves. We are truly sorry and we humbly repent. For the sake of your Son Jesus Christ, have mercy on us and forgive us; that we may delight in your will, and walk in your ways, to the glory of your Name. Amen.

Hail Mary

Hail Mary, full of grace. The Lord is with you. Blessed are you amongst women, and blessed is the fruit of your womb, Jesus. Holy Mary, Mother of God, pray for us sinners, now and at the hour of our death. Amen.

Closing Prayer

May God grant me a peaceful night and a perfect end. May the divine assistance be always with me and with all my loved ones.

Spiritual Journal

What have I done, what have I failed to do today? What have I said, what have I failed to say today? What could I do better?

Day Twenty-Four: Morning Prayer

Please take a moment of silence and quiet time.

Opening Prayer

O God, open my lips, and my mouth will proclaim your praise.

Peace and Social Justice Quote

If everyone would take only according to his needs and would leave the surplus to the needy, no one would be rich, no would be poor, and no one in misery.

— Saint Basil the Great

Prayer

Benevolent God, teach me to take what I need and not what I want so that I might share my bounty with those in need.

Please take a short period of time to contemplate the quote.

Canticle of Zechariah

Blessed are you, O God, for you have turned to your people and saved us and set us free. You have raised up for us a strong deliverer, and so you promised: age after age you proclaimed by the lips of your holy prophets that you would deliver us, calling to mind your solemn covenant. This was the promise that you made: to rescue us and free us from fear, so that we might worship you with a holy worship, in your holy presence our whole life long. In your

tender compassion, the morning sun has risen upon us – to shine on us in our darkness, to guide our feet into the paths of peace.

Our Father

Our Father, who art in heaven, hallowed be your name; your kingdom come; your will be done on earth as it is in heaven. Give us this day our daily bread; and forgive us our trespasses as we forgive those who trespass against us; and lead us not into temptation, but deliver us from evil. Amen.

Closing Prayer

May God be gracious to me, show me kindness, and fill my heart with peace.

Spiritual Journal

My peace and social justice intent for today:

Day Twenty-Four: Evening Prayer

Please take a moment of silence and quiet time.

Opening Prayer

God, come to my assistance. Holy One, make haste to help me.

Peace and Social Justice Quote

If everyone would take only according to his needs and would leave the surplus to the needy, no one would be rich, no would be poor, and no one in misery.

—Saint Basil the Great

Prayer

Benevolent God, teach me to take what I need and not what I want so that I might share my bounty with those in need.

Please take a short period of time to contemplate the quote.

Canticle of Mary

Our souls proclaim the glory of the Holy One; our spirits rejoice in God, our Savior, for you have looked with favor upon your lowly servant. You have done great things and holy is your name. You have cast down the mighty, and lifted up the lowly; you have filled the hungry with good things, and have sent the rich away empty. You have come to your children and set them free, for you have remembered your promise of mercy to our mothers and fathers, and to all your children forever.

Examination of Conscience

How have I lived according to my means to that I could leave my surplus to the needy today? What could I do better?

Act of Contrition

Most merciful God, we confess that we have sinned against you in thought, word, and deed, by what we have done, and by what we have left undone. We have not loved you with our whole heart; we have not loved our neighbors as ourselves. We are truly sorry and we humbly repent. For the sake of your Son Jesus Christ, have mercy on us and forgive us; that we may delight in your will, and walk in your ways, to the glory of your Name. Amen.

Hail Mary

Hail Mary, full of grace. The Lord is with you. Blessed are you amongst women, and blessed is the fruit of your womb, Jesus. Holy Mary, Mother of God, pray for us sinners, now and at the hour of our death. Amen.

Closing Prayer

May God grant me a peaceful night and a perfect end. May the divine assistance be always with me and with all my loved ones.

Spiritual Journal

What have I done, what have I failed to do today? What have I said, what have I failed to say today? What could I do better?

Day Twenty-Five: Morning Prayer

Opening Prayer

O God, open my lips, and my mouth will proclaim your praise.

Peace and Social Justice Quote

Indifference toward those in need is not acceptable for a Christian.

—Pope Francis

Prayer

Responsive God, often I am disinterested, unconcerned, and lack sympathy and still claim to be Christian. In the midst of the anguish, despair, and misery in our world, liberate me from my apathy.

Please take a short period of time to contemplate the quote.

Canticle of Zechariah

Blessed are you, O God, for you have turned to your people and saved us and set us free. You have raised up for us a strong deliverer, and so you promised: age after age you proclaimed by the lips of your holy prophets that you would deliver us, calling to mind your solemn covenant. This was the promise that you made: to rescue us and free us from fear, so that we might worship you with a holy worship, in your holy presence our whole life long. In your tender compassion, the morning sun has risen upon us – to shine on us in our darkness, to guide our feet into the paths of peace.

Our Father

Our Father, who art in heaven, hallowed be your name; your kingdom come; your will be done on earth as it is in heaven. Give us this day our daily bread; and forgive us our trespasses as we forgive those who trespass against us; and lead us not into temptation, but deliver us from evil. Amen.

Closing Prayer

May God be gracious to me, show me kindness, and fill my heart with peace.

Spiritual Journal

My peace and social justice intent for today:

Day Twenty-Five: Evening Prayer

Opening Prayer

God, come to my assistance. Holy One, make haste to help me.

Peace and Social Justice Quote

Indifference toward those in need is not acceptable for a Christian.
—Pope Francis

Prayer

Responsive God, often I am disinterested, unconcerned, and lack sympathy and still claim to be Christian. In the midst of the anguish, despair, and misery in our world, liberate me from my apathy.

Please take a short period of time to contemplate the quote.

Canticle of Mary

Our souls proclaim the glory of the Holy One; our spirits rejoice in God, our Savior, for you have looked with favor upon your lowly servant. You have done great things and holy is your name. You have cast down the mighty, and lifted up the lowly; you have filled the hungry with good things, and have sent the rich away empty. You have come to your children and set them free, for you have remembered your promise of mercy to our mothers and fathers, and to all your children forever.

Examination of Conscience

In what ways have I demonstrated concern for those in anguish, despair or misery so that I was not a hypocrite by claiming to be Christian while having an attitude of indifference today? What could I do better?

Act of Contrition

Most merciful God, we confess that we have sinned against you in thought, word, and deed, by what we have done, and by what we have left undone. We have not loved you with our whole heart; we have not loved our neighbors as ourselves. We are truly sorry and we humbly repent. For the sake of your Son Jesus Christ, have mercy on us and forgive us; that we may delight in your will, and walk in your ways, to the glory of your Name. Amen.

Hail Mary

Hail Mary, full of grace. The Lord is with you. Blessed are you amongst women, and blessed is the fruit of your womb, Jesus. Holy Mary, Mother of God, pray for us sinners, now and at the hour of our death. Amen.

Closing Prayer

May God grant me a peaceful night and a perfect end. May the divine assistance be always with me and with all my loved ones.

Spiritual Journal

What have I done, what have I failed to do today? What have I said, what have I failed to say today? What could I do better?

Day Twenty-Six: Morning Prayer

Please take a moment of silence and quiet time.

Opening Prayer

O God, open my lips, and my mouth will proclaim your praise.

Peace and Social Justice Quote

Give something, however small, to one in need. For it is not small to one who has nothing. Neither is it small to God, if we have given what we could.

—St. Gregory of Nazianzus

Prayer

Charitable God, free me to love others in the spirit of charity.

Please take a short period of time to contemplate the quote.

Canticle of Zechariah

Blessed are you, O God, for you have turned to your people and saved us and set us free.You have raised up for us a strong deliverer, and so you promised: age after age you proclaimed by the lips of your holy prophets that you would deliver us, calling to mind your solemn covenant. This was the promise that you made: to rescue us and free us from fear, so that we might worship you with a holy worship, in your holy presence our whole life long. In your

tender compassion, the morning sun has risen upon us – to shine on us in our darkness, to guide our feet into the paths of peace.

Our Father

Our Father, who art in heaven, hallowed be your name; your kingdom come; your will be done on earth as it is in heaven. Give us this day our daily bread; and forgive us our trespasses as we forgive those who trespass against us; and lead us not into temptation, but deliver us from evil. Amen.

Closing Prayer

May God be gracious to me, show me kindness, and fill my heart with peace.

Spiritual Journal

My peace and social justice intent for today:

Day Twenty-Six: Evening Prayer

Please take a moment of silence and quiet time.

Opening Prayer

God, come to my assistance. Holy One, make haste to help me.

Peace and Social Justice Quote

Give something, however small, to one in need. For it is not small to one who has nothing. Neither is it small to God, if we have given what we could.

—St. Gregory of Nazianzus

Prayer

Charitable God, free me to love others in the spirit of charity.

Please take a short period of time to contemplate the quote.

Canticle of Mary

Our souls proclaim the glory of the Holy One; our spirits rejoice in God, our Savior, for you have looked with favor upon your lowly servant. You have done great things and holy is your name. You have cast down the mighty, and lifted up the lowly; you have filled the hungry with good things, and have sent the rich away empty. You have come to your children and set them free, for you have remembered your promise of mercy to our mothers and fathers, and to all your children forever.

Examination of Conscience

In what ways have I demonstrated concern for those in anguish, despair or misery so that I was not a hypocrite by claiming to be Christian while having an attitude of indifference today? What could I do better?

Act of Contrition

Most merciful God, we confess that we have sinned against you in thought, word, and deed, by what we have done, and by what we have left undone. We have not loved you with our whole heart; we have not loved our neighbors as ourselves. We are truly sorry and we humbly repent. For the sake of your Son Jesus Christ, have mercy on us and forgive us; that we may delight in your will, and walk in your ways, to the glory of your Name. Amen.

Hail Mary

Hail Mary, full of grace. The Lord is with you. Blessed are you amongst women, and blessed is the fruit of your womb, Jesus. Holy Mary, Mother of God, pray for us sinners, now and at the hour of our death. Amen.

Closing Prayer

May God grant me a peaceful night and a perfect end. May the divine assistance be always with me and with all my loved ones.

Spiritual Journal

What have I done, what have I failed to do today? What have I said, what have I failed to say today? What could I do better?

Day Twenty-Seven: Morning Prayer

Please take a moment of silence and quiet time.

Opening Prayer

O God, open my lips, and my mouth will proclaim your praise.

Peace and Social Justice Quote

Once the demands of necessity and propriety have been met, the rest belongs to the poor.

—Pope Leo XIII

Prayer

Generous God, release me from the bondage of selfishness and inspire me to lavish the poor with what is equitably theirs by your sacred design.

Please take a short period of time to contemplate the quote.

Canticle of Zechariah

Blessed are you, O God, for you have turned to your people and saved us and set us free. You have raised up for us a strong deliverer, and so you promised: age after age you proclaimed by the lips of your holy prophets that you would deliver us, calling to mind your solemn covenant. This was the promise that you made: to rescue us and free us from fear, so that we might worship you with a holy worship, in your holy presence our whole life long. In your

tender compassion, the morning sun has risen upon us – to shine on us in our darkness, to guide our feet into the paths of peace.

Our Father

Our Father, who art in heaven, hallowed be your name; your kingdom come; your will be done on earth as it is in heaven. Give us this day our daily bread; and forgive us our trespasses as we forgive those who trespass against us; and lead us not into temptation, but deliver us from evil. Amen.

Closing Prayer

May God be gracious to me, show me kindness, and fill my heart with peace.

Spiritual Journal

My peace and social justice intent for today:

Day Twenty-Seven: Evening Prayer

Please take a moment of silence and quiet time.

Opening Prayer

God, come to my assistance. Holy One, make haste to help me.

Peace and Social Justice Quote

Once the demands of necessity and propriety have been met, the rest belongs to the poor.

—Pope Leo XIII

Prayer

Generous God, release me from the bondage of selfishness and inspire me to lavish the poor with what is equitably theirs by your sacred design.

Please take a short period of time to contemplate the quote.

Canticle of Mary

Our souls proclaim the glory of the Holy One; our spirits rejoice in God, our Savior, for you have looked with favor upon your lowly servant. You have done great things and holy is your name. You have cast down the mighty, and lifted up the lowly; you have filled the hungry with good things, and have sent the rich away empty. You have come to your children and set them free, for you have

remembered your promise of mercy to our mothers and fathers, and to all your children forever.

Examination of Conscience

After the demands of necessity and propriety have been met, did I give the rest to the poverty-stricken today? What could I do better?

Act of Contrition

Most merciful God, we confess that we have sinned against you in thought, word, and deed, by what we have done, and by what we have left undone. We have not loved you with our whole heart; we have not loved our neighbors as ourselves. We are truly sorry and we humbly repent. For the sake of your Son Jesus Christ, have mercy on us and forgive us; that we may delight in your will, and walk in your ways, to the glory of your Name. Amen.

Hail Mary

Hail Mary, full of grace. The Lord is with you. Blessed are you amongst women, and blessed is the fruit of your womb, Jesus. Holy Mary, Mother of God, pray for us sinners, now and at the hour of our death. Amen.

Closing Prayer

May God grant me a peaceful night and a perfect end. May the divine assistance be always with me and with all my loved ones.

Spiritual Journal

What have I done, what have I failed to do today? What have I said, what have I failed to say today? What could I do better?

Day Twenty-Eight: Morning Prayer

Please take a moment of silence and quiet time.

Opening Prayer

O God, open my lips, and my mouth will proclaim your praise.

Peace and Social Justice Quote

If there are poor on the moon, we will go there too.

—St. Teresa

Prayer

Sharing God, create in me the yearning to follow your ways by giving what I am able to a friend, foe, or stranger who has nothing.

Please take a short period of time to contemplate the quote.

Canticle of Zechariah

Blessed are you, O God, for you have turned to your people and saved us and set us free. You have raised up for us a strong deliverer, and so you promised: age after age you proclaimed by the lips of your holy prophets that you would deliver us, calling to mind your solemn covenant. This was the promise that you made: to rescue us and free us from fear, so that we might worship you with a holy worship, in your holy presence our whole life long. In your tender compassion, the morning sun has risen upon us – to shine on us in our darkness, to guide our feet into the paths of peace.

Our Father

Our Father, who art in heaven, hallowed be your name; your kingdom come; your will be done on earth as it is in heaven. Give us this day our daily bread; and forgive us our trespasses as we forgive those who trespass against us; and lead us not into temptation, but deliver us from evil. Amen.

Closing Prayer

May God be gracious to me, show me kindness, and fill my heart with peace.

Spiritual Journal

My peace and social justice intent for today:

Day Twenty-Eight: Evening Prayer

Please take a moment of silence and quiet time.

Opening Prayer

God, come to my assistance. Holy One, make haste to help me.

Peace and Social Justice Quote

If there are poor on the moon, we will go there too.

—St. Teresa

Prayer

Sharing God, create in me the yearning to follow your ways by giving what I am able to a friend, foe, or stranger who has nothing.

Please take a short period of time to contemplate the quote.

Canticle of Mary

Our souls proclaim the glory of the Holy One; our spirits rejoice in God, our Savior, for you have looked with favor upon your lowly servant. You have done great things and holy is your name. You have cast down the mighty, and lifted up the lowly; you have filled the hungry with good things, and have sent the rich away empty. You have come to your children and set them free, for you have remembered your promise of mercy to our mothers and fathers, and to all your children forever.

Examination of Conscience

Have I done everything possible to help those who are impoverished today? What could I do better?

Act of Contrition

Most merciful God, we confess that we have sinned against you in thought, word, and deed, by what we have done, and by what we have left undone. We have not loved you with our whole heart; we have not loved our neighbors as ourselves. We are truly sorry and we humbly repent. For the sake of your Son Jesus Christ, have mercy on us and forgive us; that we may delight in your will, and walk in your ways, to the glory of your Name. Amen.

Hail Mary

Hail Mary, full of grace. The Lord is with you. Blessed are you amongst women, and blessed is the fruit of your womb, Jesus. Holy Mary, Mother of God, pray for us sinners, now and at the hour of our death. Amen.

Closing Prayer

May God grant me a peaceful night and a perfect end. May the divine assistance be always with me and with all my loved ones.

Spiritual Journal

What have I done, what have I failed to do today? What have I said, what have I failed to say today? What could I do better?

Day Twenty-Nine: Morning Prayer

Please take a moment of silence and quiet time.

Opening Prayer

O God, open my lips, and my mouth will proclaim your praise.

Peace and Social Justice Quote

Christ invites us not to fear persecution because, believe me, brothers and sisters, whoever decides for the poor must endure the same fate as the poor, and in El Salvador we know what the fate of the poor really means to disappear, to be tortured, to be imprisoned, and to be found dead.

—Archbishop Oscar Romero

Prayer

Brave God, aid me in responding to your call and invitation to a commitment to be in solidarity with poor and the courage to endure their fate.

Please take a short period of time to contemplate the quote.

Canticle of Zechariah

Blessed are you, O God, for you have turned to your people and saved us and set us free.You have raised up for us a strong deliverer, and so you promised: age after age you proclaimed by the lips of your holy prophets that you would deliver us, calling to mind your solemn covenant. This was the promise that you made: to rescue us and free us from fear, so that we might worship you with a holy worship, in your holy presence our whole life long. In your tender compassion, the morning sun has risen upon us – to shine on us in our darkness, to guide our feet into the paths of peace.

Our Father

Our Father, who art in heaven, hallowed be your name; your kingdom come; your will be done on earth as it is in heaven. Give us this day our daily bread; and forgive us our trespasses as we forgive those who trespass against us; and lead us not into temptation, but deliver us from evil. Amen.

Closing Prayer

May God be gracious to me, show me kindness, and fill my heart with peace.

Spiritual Journal

My peace and social justice intent for today:

Day Twenty-Nine: Evening Prayer

Please take a moment of silence and quiet time.

Opening Prayer

God, come to my assistance. Holy One, make haste to help me.

Peace and Social Justice Quote

Christ invites us not to fear persecution because, believe me, brothers and sisters, whoever decides for the poor must endure the same fate as the poor, and in El Salvador we know what the fate of the poor really means: to disappear, to be tortured, to be imprisoned, and to be found dead.

—Archbishop Oscar Romero

Prayer

Brave God, aid me in responding to your call and invitation to a commitment to be in solidarity with poor and the courage to endure their fate.

Please take a short period of time to contemplate the quote.

Canticle of Mary

Our souls proclaim the glory of the Holy One; our spirits rejoice in God, our Savior, for you have looked with favor upon your lowly servant. you have done great things and holy is your name. You have cast down the mighty, and lifted up the lowly; you have filled the hungry with good things, and have sent the rich away empty. You have come to your children and set them free, for you have remembered your promise of mercy to our mothers and fathers, and to all your children forever.

Examination of Conscience

Have I done everything possible to help those who are impoverished today? What could I do better?

Act of Contrition

Most merciful God, we confess that we have sinned against you in thought, word, and deed, by what we have done, and by what we have left undone. We have not loved you with our whole heart; we have not loved our neighbors as ourselves. We are truly sorry and we humbly repent. For the sake of your Son Jesus Christ, have mercy on us and forgive us; that we may delight in your will, and walk in your ways, to the glory of your Name. Amen.

Hail Mary

Hail Mary, full of grace. The Lord is with you. Blessed are you amongst women, and blessed is the fruit of your womb, Jesus. Holy Mary, Mother of God, pray for us sinners, now and at the hour of our death. Amen.

Closing Prayer

May God grant me a peaceful night and a perfect end. May the divine assistance be always with me and with all my loved ones.

Spiritual Journal

What have I done, what have I failed to do today? What have I said, what have I failed to say today? What could I do better?

Day Thirty: Morning Prayer

Please take a moment of silence and quiet time.

Opening Prayer

O God, open my lips, and my mouth will proclaim your praise.

Peace and Social Justice Quote

Every person is Jesus in disguise.

—St. Teresa

Prayer

Merciful God, help me to recognize you in every person I encounter.

Please take a short period of time to contemplate the quote.

Canticle of Zechariah

Blessed are you, O God, for you have turned to your people and saved us and set us free. You have raised up for us a strong deliverer, and so you promised: age after age you proclaimed by the lips of your holy prophets that you would deliver us, calling to mind your solemn covenant. This was the promise that you made: to rescue us and free us from fear, so that we might worship you with a holy worship, in your holy presence our whole life long. In your tender compassion, the morning sun has risen upon us – to shine on us in our darkness, to guide our feet into the paths of peace.

Our Father

Our Father, who art in heaven, hallowed be your name; your kingdom come; your will be done on earth as it is in heaven. Give us this day our daily bread; and forgive us our trespasses as we forgive those who trespass against us; and lead us not into temptation, but deliver us from evil. Amen.

Closing Prayer

May God be gracious to me, show me kindness, and fill my heart with peace.

Spiritual Journal

My peace and social justice intent for today:

Day Thirty: Evening Prayer

Please take a moment of silence and quiet time.

Opening Prayer

God, come to my assistance. Holy One, make haste to help me.

Peace and Social Justice Quote

Every person is Jesus in disguise.

—St. Teresa

Prayer

Merciful God, help me to recognize you in every person I encounter.

Please take a short period of time to contemplate the quote.

Canticle of Mary

Our souls proclaim the glory of the Holy One; our spirits rejoice in God, our Savior, for you have looked with favor upon your lowly servant. You have done great things and holy is your name. you have cast down the mighty, and lifted up the lowly; you have filled the hungry with good things, and have sent the rich away empty. You have come to your children and set them free, for you have remembered your promise of mercy to our mothers and fathers, and to all your children forever.

Examination of Conscience

Have I recognized God in every person I encountered today? What could I do better?

Act of Contrition

Most merciful God, we confess that we have sinned against you in thought, word, and deed, by what we have done, and by what we have left undone. We have not loved you with our whole heart; we have not loved our neighbors as ourselves. We are truly sorry and we humbly repent. For the sake of your Son Jesus Christ, have mercy on us and forgive us; that we may delight in your will, and walk in your ways, to the glory of your Name. Amen.

Hail Mary

Hail Mary, full of grace. The Lord is with you. Blessed are you amongst women, and blessed is the fruit of your womb, Jesus. Holy Mary, Mother of God, pray for us sinners, now and at the hour of our death. Amen.

Closing Prayer

May God grant me a peaceful night and a perfect end. May the divine assistance be always with me and with all my loved ones.

Spiritual Journal

What have I done, what have I failed to do today? What have I said, what have I failed to say today? What could I do better?

References

Brainy Quotes www.brainyquote.com

Catholic quotations www.catholicquotations.com

Catholic Charities of St. Paul and Minneapolis www.//cctwincities.
org/education-advocacy/catholic-social-teaching/

Catholic quotations www.catholicquotations.com

Canticle of Zechariah and Canticle of Mary: Benson, R. (2000).
Venite: A book of daily prayer. New York. Penguin Putman Inc.

Acknowledgements

Thanks and appreciation to my two editors, Pat Sullivan and Karen Campbell, for their sage editing wisdom and creative insight.

About The Author

Lou Bordisso is a Roman Catholic Companion with the Ecumenical Order of Charity. He has been a licensed marriage, family, and child therapists 1987 providing individual and couples counseling, spiritual and pastoral care. Bordisso is also the author of the book, Sex, Celibacy, and Priesthood. He holds an Ed.D. from the University of San Francisco in Counseling and Educational Psychology, a Masters of Marriage and Family Counseling also from the University of San Francisco, and an M.Div. from the Franciscan School of Theology at the Graduate School of Theology in Berkeley, California.

Since his diagnosis with both Younger Onset Alzheimer's and Lewy Body Dementias, Bordisso has retired from his secular employment as a forensic mental health provider and his religious ministry as a spiritual care hospice chaplain. During retirement, much of his time continues with peace and social justice, especially among homeless men and women. In addition, he advocates for and speaks nationwide for Alzheimer's and related memory impairments.

www.ingramcontent.com/pod-product-compliance
Lightning Source LLC
Chambersburg PA
CBHW031135090426
42738CB00008B/1099